Images for Change

The Transformation of Society

Rosemary Luling Haughton

L.-A. Cunningham

Notre Dame – 1998

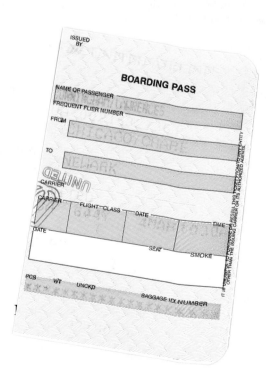

The Publisher gratefully acknowledges use of the following. Excerpt from *Rosencrantz and Guildenstern Are Dead* by Tom Stoppard. Copyright 1988. Used by permission of Grove/Atlantic, Inc. Excerpts from *The Architecture of Complexity* by Lucien Kroll (translated by Peter Blundell Jones). Copyright 1987. Used by permission of MIT Press, Cambridge, MA. Excerpt from song lyrics of *No Going Back* by Sandra Kerr. Excerpt from *Places of the Soul* by Christopher Day. Copyright 1993. Thorsons San Francisco. Excerpt from *The Dispossessed* by Ursula LeGuin. Copyright 1976. Harper-Collins Publishers.

Jacket design by Cindy Dunne

Library of Congress Cataloging-in-Publication Data

Haughton, Rosemary.
    Images for change : the transformation of society / Rosemary Luling Haughton.
      p. cm.
    ISBN 0-8091-0490-3 (cloth : alk. paper)
    1. Social change. 2. Social structure. 3. Hospitality. 4. Architecture—Philosophy. 5. Spatial behavior. I. Title.
HM101.H379   1997
303.4—DC21   97-24851
                                                         CIP

Published by Paulist Press
997 Macarthur Boulevard
Mahwah, New Jersey 07430

Printed and bound in the
United States of America

Contents

Appreciations

Books are always the product of many minds, hands and lives beyond that of the author.

This one owes its existence in print to Ruth Pelley, whose computer literacy forgave my illiteracy and whose hospitality to the text and its many revisions ensured it actually got finished.

The book owes its very life, also, to those with whom, over many years, I learned about hospitality: my own family, who carry on the tradition; the gallant visionary community of Lothlorien in Galloway; and all the people of Wellspring House in Massachusetts with whom I shared a vision that became a reality and is still a vision.

Preface

A building is not a pile of wood, nor is it a structure defined by architects or archeologists. Our buildings are human places in human times, actors in human dramas—our cottages, apartments skyscrapers, churches, silos, factories, tree houses, nuclear plants, as well as the packing-box kips of the homeless. All these dwelling places are participants in human history.

We can envision our worlds, our collective pasts and our futures, as human habitations that we create together. Through this image we can come to see the social and economic structures within which we live—and how to change them. That is the fundamental insight behind this remarkable book in which Rosemary Luling Haughton presents a new, humanist theory based on the concept of hospitality and centered on imagination and community cooperation.

The inspiration for the book came when she learned of the work of the Belgian architect Lucien Kroll, particularly Kroll's conversion of old buildings to new uses. She writes of Kroll's transformation of a barn to a church:

> There was a double vision of the old identity and the new one, never coinciding, yet present in the same space. The purposes and meanings of the past were not mere memory but still there, to be apprehended in the present, while the new use, and the means to it, established themselves without compromise or nostalgia. Kroll had reimagined the use of the space out of an awareness of its old use.

With this image of the old habitation transformed to new human use, we see life as a process in time. The community becomes the architect of its future, out of its inheritance from the past.

For Rosemary the image of a building is not simply a useful metaphor but a way of seeing the world. In our dwelling places we can see the structure of our lives, if we only look. What is there for us to see in the unadorned straight lines of modern factories and office buildings into which workers come and go at regimented hours, separated from the lives of their communities? What is there to learn from schoolrooms shut off from the life and work of the adult world and even the lives of the students? What is there to learn about ourselves from shopping malls that close out the weather and the daytime sky and the starlit night, where individuals are strangers in the flow of a crowd?

We can see ourselves in the neighborhoods we inhabit. Are there people sitting out on front stoops chatting and laughing? Are there inhospitable closed gates, doormen, locks and silences? The places we inhabit help us discover the structures of our collective lives.

Rosemary uses the image of a building to open the door to imagination. Do we see rotten floorboards? What is underneath? Are there windows we can punch through, magic casements that allow a vision of the future? Kindling imagination is essential to any philosophy of change that places responsibility for creating the future, not in the hands of an elite few but in the hands of ordinary people who must make the new community out of their own pasts. A humanist philosophy of hospitality is radically democratic because the source of change is situated in the places where people live, not in the corridors of legislature or presidential palace.

Hospitality is the name of a relationship of care and respect of participation and democracy. It has its roots in the distant human past in the relationship between host and guest, in the act of opening one's home and community to others. But opening one's community to others requires changing the structures that have kept the community divided into the insiders and outsiders, the "haves" and "have-nots." Hospitality requires change. In showing this, Rosemary contrasts hospitality with charity.

Charity, she writes, preserves the existing social structure and its inequalities while voluntarily bandaging some of the "unfortunates." Charity—whether individual contribution or the government charity of welfare—cannot solve the problem of homelessness or unemployment, for it leaves intact the very structures that are sources of those misfortunes. An economic structure designed to run at five per cent unemployment cannot, by its nature, offer jobs to all who want them. A commercial health care structure designed to put bottom-line profits and interests of stockholders first, by its very nature, cut back on health care. The market structure for housing, based on what the highest bidder will pay for private property will, by its very nature, deprive many people of shelter simply because the prices will exceed their ability to buy or to rent. Charity does not provide a way to solve the serious problem and, in fact, charity (whether government or individual) defines and solves the social problems by labeling people as the problem—the homeless are the problem rather than the social and economic structures. And yet the social, political and economic structures themselves are at the root of the problems.

In contrast, hospitality is about change—even radical, structural change—that comes out of the practical imagination of people committed to a collective vision. Because of these things, it needs an interpretation in practice. The philosophy of hospitality finds its interpretation in the practices of Wellspring House, where Rosemary lives and works.

Wellspring House was founded in 1981, when Rosemary and a group of friends came together, pooled slender resources to buy a venerable house in Gloucester, on Cape Ann in Massachusetts. There they began their experiment in hospitality. The house had been built in 1649 by some of the earliest English settlers in the region, in a style common to the time, with a massive frame of oak sills and beams, and at the center, a great chimney that served the fireplaces of the household.

The vision of the founders was expressed in the word *hospitality.* In the beginning, they opened the home to people in crisis—the elderly, teenagers, families. Within a year or two, homelessness was recognized as a public problem in the United States and it became clear that the homeless needed a basic kind of care. Wellspring became a place of hospitality for homeless families (most of them women with young children). The house was home not only to these homeless, but to Rosemary and the other founding members. They shared the home with families (and still share it). They shared both the house and the grounds, for there were always vegetable gardens, flower beds, lawns, rock gardens and areas for children to play.

Sheltering is necessary, but it is not a solution to homelessness. In a few years. Wellspring moved to provide affordable housing, first by rehabilitating houses in Gloucester, then, in 1988, by forming a community land trust to provide affordable home ownership on land held in trust. Wellspring House was growing roots in the community and changing the community environment, in company with people of the community.

There have been many ways that Wellspring has practiced hospitality with the people of Cape Ann. In 1990, a research project was begun with eighty formerly homeless women. The research was designed to discover how the experience of homelessness had changed them, where their lives were at present, and what their hopes and dreams were. The result was the study, "We Are Like You," and it served as the basis for a 1991 community symposium that set the direction of future work.

Over the next five years, the experiment in hospitality drew in people from all walks of life in Gloucester and other communities on Cape Ann, as Wellspring House began new projects—in housing education and local economic development, and in incubating community project that then took on lives of their own.

There are sacred rites of the household that express care for others. Some mark important events in people's lives—a cake and a song for birthdays, a celebration when a family in the shelter find permanent housing. Others mark the sacred cycles of the seasons, such as a women's winter solstice celebration. In others, Wellspring invites the larger community to play hostess to itself in a grand, collaborative act of hospitality and solidarity. In the summer of 1996, there was a festival called "Broadway Under the Stars." The use of an oceanside property was donated for the event. Volunteers came together to produce this community event, working as musicians, sound technicians, dancers, electricians, cooks, organizers and jacks-and-jills-of-all-trades.

The house itself changed with the addition of the Veronese Community Education Resource Center, built in response to community needs though a massive common effort. Its various courses and events focus on education for people working to escape poverty, and on many justice issues. In January, 1996, Wellspring House sponsored a community forum on assessing the future, with the goal of engaging "residents and friends of the Cape Ann community to research, imagine and act toward a community that will become self-sustaining."

Wellspring's history is an experiment in hospitality, as Gandhi's *satyagraha* was an experiment in truth. It is an experiment that is essential to the political philosophy presented in this book by Rosemary Luling Haughton, otherwise it would only be a utopian dream, not a practical and tested method of change. Wellspring House provides the background for putting this principle into practice, but the contribution this book makes to the political philosophy of hospitality is the stirring of our practical imagination.

Rosemary stirs the imagination in several ways, most importantly by teaching the reader to use the central image of a dwelling place. She also uses novels and history. One of the novels Rosemary discusses is Ursula LeGuin's *The Dispossessed,* a novel about an anarchist society on a moon called Annares that circles the democratic capitalist society A–1o, one of the nations on the planet from which the anarchists were exiled. Anarres has no central government, and it operates on the basis of what Rosemary calls hospitality in the sense that all who live there receive what they need for living, not only food and shelter, but (if they like) art, sport and sociability. Though their system has serious flaws, they are raised to live in terms of the good of the whole, rather than individual good. Rosemary writes that these anarchists were exiled not so much because they presented an actual threat to the democratic and capitalist structures, but because they questioned the basic assumption that the way of the capitalist democracy is natural, that is, inevitable.

That is what this book questions—that our present way, our

present dwelling place, is natural and inevitable. Rosemary does not give us a plan for the community we should reach as a goal. Like LeGuin, she opens magic windows that let us see our present and past (as LeGuin's Anarres looks across at the planet Urras as its past, and the planet Urras looks out at its moon as a possible future). The goal is a hospitable community and world, but ones that are envisioned and constructed from the ground up, in thousands of communities.

In giving us a politics of hospitality, Rosemary makes a major contribution to humanist moral and political theory. As I understand it, hospitality is a politics of care. Any system of humanist politics must be based on a transformed understanding of social relationships, but the transformation must come from experiments in changing the social, political and economic orders together. It requires a way to know what the structures of the society and community are in order to criticize them, in order to know how one's own experience is constructed within those structures.

The humanist politics of hospitality is one of welcome and equality, in which people of a community participate in changing their collective life. This system of politics lets us imagine ways of change that go beyond existing governmental or market structures. It stirs the practical imagination of women, children and men, or rich and poor. It opens magic windows for people to see the possibilities for new life. It frees the powerful from the shackles of the structures within which they exercise their power. In these ways, it is a humanist politics that offers hospitality to all of us.

Kathryn Pyne Addelson
Smith College

Introduction

*T*his book is written for people who have a hard time feeling hopeful about the future. A writer's job is to reflect back feelings, thoughts, insights (even fantasies) that are shared by many. If my reaction to life at the end of the twentieth century were unique there would be little point in putting it in print, but it is not. If I experience a constant underlying depression about what is happening to the earth and its people, so do millions of others. All our personal experiences of success or failure, health, growth, relationship, are affected by awareness of changes so vast and uncontrollable that one's own small circle of sanity and affection seems liable to be overwhelmed. We can, and do, keep it all outside direct consciousness for much of the time, in order to function, experience happiness, make decisions, *live*. But it is there, not so much as despair—the future possibilities are too unclear for that—but rather as alternating waves of grief, fear, rage, unbelief, panic, hope, resignation, cynicism—and back to the beginning and so on.

This book proposes a response to this experience that is both personal and structural.

It is personal both in the sense that it develops out of my own specific experience and that it proposes a way of thinking and imagining that can allow the individual to deal with contemporary reality in a way that makes both hope and appropriate action possible.

It is structural in the sense that it provides tools for a critique of existing structures and a way of imagining realistic alternatives.

My proposed response is offered in the form of a strong central set of images, which are architectural and therefore easily

1

evoked, and it will be clear that the architectural images are important as just literal images of habitations that affect and express all human life—but also, importantly, as metonyms for all of human life. One aspect—the habitation—indicates the wider whole or makes its nature more accessible. So the architectural images are also political: by using these images, both literally and metonymically, I am able to present ideas about political structure that cannot be presented abstractly, or at least would not be very persuasive that way.

The thesis—the political theory if you will—presented through the use of architectural images is that the concept of hospitality is a key to a different, and yet very traditional, way to the making of personal, communal, social and political decisions. Hospitality sets out criteria for decisions that are very different from those usually regarded as relevant, and the differences and the problems they raise are explored in this book.

The notion of hospitality also indicates another key concern in this writing, which is the relationship between continuity and change. These turn out to be not so much antithetical as essentially interdependent, and the use of architectural images makes this clear.

Hospitality as a theme also emerges as a necessary one for myself, because through all my life that has been a central concern. Making homes and sharing them has been my calling—as a wife and mother for whom hospitality was an explicit criterion for family decisions about the use (and abuse) of domestic spaces, and as a member of two successive and very different communities, both of them dedicated to the practice of hospitality. These experiences both therefore obliged me to wrestle with the nature, the purpose and the limits of hospitality and the implications of that for the design of living spaces large and small.

In the case of the second community, the one in which I now live, the implications of hospitality as a criterion have been taken further in terms of the creation of affordable housing, economic development and education that includes a social and feminist critique of the structures (literal and metaphorical) that inhibit hospitality and constrict lives. In this context exploration of the political implications of hospitality have therefore been undertaken here in some depth as a practical necessity but at the same time as a religious and theological one.

In this introduction I shall explore some of the reasons why it seemed important to undertake the writing of this book, and the background against which that writing has to be understood, for we live at a time when we have lost, or are in danger of losing, most of the structures which traditionally made it possible for people to move through the vicissitudes of their own lives with some certainty that they were just that—personal struggles, successes, failures and hopes. These events could unfold within systems that, in spite of occasional war or natural disaster, did not expect to change very much. Cultures differ, but within each the expectations have been reasonably constant for good or ill for a very long time—and this even though there had, in fact, been many a cultural upheaval and change. These had happened far apart, slowly, or long ago, and the perception of continuity and stability, if delusive, was powerful. It was what made disaster bearable, or at least survivable, because there was a clear image of what was "normal," to which one hoped to return.

In a recent movie, an old woman refers to a time in her youth when, though away from her soldier husband, she did not have affairs with other men. "You didn't, if you were married, in those days." A young man responds, "I think I've read about that." The comment is intended to be ironic but it makes the point. Class, family, property, belief, were *there,* they had "always" been there; the expectations, and the sanctions were clear. Even in the breach, the rules provided a way to know where one stood. Now most of that has gone. In less than one century we have experienced two world wars, several others almost as destructive, the holocaust, "the bomb," the rise and collapse of the Soviet system, the Chinese revolution and re-revolution, the end of explicit colonialism but the neo-colonial creation of a "third world" of economically dependent and impoverished nations, the successful control of world economy (and therefore governments) by multi-national corporations, itself linked to the massive pollution by industrial and agricultural chemicals that is endangering the earth's life systems, the spread of AIDS, and the vast sub-cultures and sub-economies of drugs. All this in three generations.

Also in three or four generations the basis of our thinking about physical reality itself has been shifted. From a Newtonian cosmology in which the universe is perceived as a vast machine (with or without a divine mechanic in charge) which at least in principle we can understand and control, we have been shoved into a strange universe in which energy and matter are interchangeable, and in which reality can be something created by our observations and by decisions we make. And—worse still—we are required somehow to integrate this very disconcerting perception of reality with the old Newtonian perception that in practice governs our ordinary experience, where apples continue to fall from trees whether we notice them or not and the earth circles the sun regardless of our observations.

How do we deal with this? How do we vote? How do we make sensible decisions? Where do we look for salvation (if any)?

In this kind of world, how do you label your attitudes? Are you Conservative? Liberal? Left wing? Right wing? Radical? Most of us identify with some such label (with whatever hesitations and modifiers we find necessary to our self-respect) whether we are thinking about politics, or religion, or art, or economics, or education or whatever. And the label we choose for ourselves (however tentative) reflects a desire (however hazy) to make things better than they are. One end of the spectrum reflects the feeling that, as this disastrous century draws to a close, so much has been destroyed that our only hope is to preserve and reinforce such remnants of tried-and-true traditions as we can, lest we descend into total chaos. The other end responds to the feeling that the wreck is so near total that any remaining traditional structures—economic, governmental, theological, familial and others—are not only useless but represent the remains of systems that caused the wreck in the first place, so the only hope is in their abolition. Probably most of us hover somewhere in between the extremes, because in fact we can identify with the *feelings* that lead to even the most extreme views, though we may reject the views. So how do we, ordinary people, mostly with at least remnants of religious beliefs, respond with honesty and sanity to the situation in which we find ourselves? On what premises do we base our decisions—political, personal, religious? How do we even *think* about life, since with the collapse of so much that seemed secure we have also lost confidence in the possibility of thinking clearly and coherently, beyond certain narrowly personal limits? And even those limits appear questionable when we look at them carefully.

For instance, what kind of education do I want for my children or grandchildren? The answer to that depends on what kind of world they will have to deal with. I can't assume that what seemed a "good" education in the 1990s will be "good" for the twenty-first century. (Was it even good for the 1980s?) What about career choices? Type of home? What kinds of jobs will there be in twenty years? Does it even make sense to have children, when they will conceivably have to wear long sleeves, huge hats and dark glasses whenever they go out in the sun lest they get skin cancer or become as blind as the sheep in Chile and the reindeer in Lapland are already becoming? In the religious sphere, is my church really held together by anything stronger than the need for a supportive community? But isn't a supportive community a basic need anyway? All the personal questions hinge on the global ones, and on the ultimate ones. Why is there an earth? Why are there people? What is life? What is God—if such a notion makes sense? What on earth is it all about anyway?

The purpose of this book, as I suggested, is to ask: How can we *think* about life? Is there a way of *imagining* that can give us some kind of grasp of the nature of the issues so that we know what we are doing?

"Thinking" means language, and language requires images. Images carry our meaning; they make connections without which we can't know what we know. Images are so embedded in our language that we often don't even realize they are there. I say someone is *kind* and forget that word means the person behaves as if he or she was *kin* to me, with all the implications of the importance of blood ties in our history. I call a statement *profound* without connecting it to the profundity of the ocean. I can talk about "higher" aspirations or "lower" appetites and have to stop and think before I recognize that these descriptions come out of a Greek philosophy that categorized human feelings in that way, so that "higher" is nearer to the gods, and "lower" to the underworld. Images are what enable us to think, so changing our thinking means changing our images. We need to *imagine* differently. My choice of architectural images is certainly not the only possible one, but they are powerful, realistic and truthful and also uniquely appropriate, as I hope to show.

The image is of a house, a building, a structure, a home—what we live in—and it will provide the basis (what you build on) for reimagining the reality of the present and therefore the future, which always involves reimagining the past also, as we reimagine and therefore reinterpret our future.

This image is one we use all the time. We talk about structures—of living, of education, of society. We even talk about (or at least hear about) strange things in modern physics such as "dissipative structures" that reverse entropy. We talk about "building" character, career, community, confidence. We talk (in more elite circles) about "constructs," meaning mental arrangements of connected concepts. We "lay foundations" for enterprises and careers, we "build" or "break" walls between classes, ethnic groups, philosophies, individuals, life-styles. We "open doors" to opportunities and possibilities, and close them to hostility or fear; we open windows too, and let in "the fresh air" of new ideas; we start a career "on the ground floor," then climb to higher "levels" of achievement, but are stopped by "ceilings" of various kinds. We devise "shelters" from tax demands and other wild beasts. Once, great dynastic families were referred to metonymically as "houses," and so, still, are some banks, publishers and fashion designers. So it goes on. It is hard to imagine how we could talk about human life, individually or collectively, without images concerned with structures of some kind. In cultures without permanent buildings the images may be different, but they still refer to the structures in which people live: in Hebrew scripture the prophet Isaiah evokes a pastoral past when, to express hospitality, he speaks of "widening the tent," meaning we have to move the tent pegs further out so as to accommodate more people. Here, strikingly, hospitality and structure are linked by attitudes and decisions about how to live socially. These are the issues I shall be exploring.

The image of a building also provides us with ominous images for disaster. The very word *insecure* evokes loosening slates and crumbling masonry, and when we talk of the "collapse" of a career or a business the image is one of a fallen building, with all its pathos of the visible destruction (de-struction) of something carefully built to contain and support a whole life. A "collapsed" structure may, perhaps, be rebuilt, but the ultimate word *ruin* is powerful in its tragic finality. It may be the ruin of personal beauty, of fortune, intelligence, a national economy, or a great bank: if they are "ruined" there is no recovery. Something else may be cherished in their place, even if it be only a photograph or a memoir; perhaps even a replica may be attempted, but still a ruin is a structure destroyed beyond repair. Though it may be preserved in its ruined form for the sake of its nostalgic beauty or historical interest it is no longer a human habitation.

Images of building express our awareness of what is happening to ourselves and our culture but also, as I hope to demonstrate, help us to analyze it, reflect on it and make decisions based on it.

Most of the time we don't do this. As I suggested, we use images without thinking about how or why we do it, or what the images imply about our worldview or our attitudes. Our minds are accustomed to thinking and feeling with images and we seldom stop to make conscious connections. But it is becoming essential to be aware of the implications of the images we use. The reason for this has to do with what I have already suggested—the increased speed of change in the past century, change that is still accelerating.

Rapid change in our time is a given, and in many ways we

try to adjust to it. But at a certain point the process produces not just a progression in terms of speed and quantity of change but also changes in the quality of the experience. The human mind, accustomed to the effort to adjust to change by using familiar, though sharpened, tools of imagery and analysis, finds itself increasingly out of touch with the nature of the experience of change itself. This can lead to a kind of imaginative shut-down: for survival, the human mind screens out the excess of information it cannot deal with and tries to focus on what is immediate and familiar. One example of this is the way the idealism and activism of younger people in the sixties, who thought they knew what needed to be changed and could change it, gave way to what came to be called the "'me' generation" of people who concentrated on their own careers and relationships not only because of the failure of the '60s "causes" but because the issues turned out to be so much more complex and intransigent than they had imagined. It was all too much, and to confront it seemed like heading into frustration and madness. Better do what you can, where you are, and hope for the best. This kind of imaginative paralysis, and the danger it poses for the culture as a whole, has been explored by psychologists and philosophers, worried over by social workers, teachers and parents, evaded by politicians, industrialists and business schools. And there are signs that this is giving way to a sober realization that in practice we can't close out the realities of climatic and economic change, and that concentration on personal success is not only impractical but spiritually destructive. Many are searching for a different way, but many of these ways are as destructive as the paralysis itself. That is why it is so important to find a truthful, practical, internally and externally coherent way to break the imaginative paralysis, to begin to move, to perceive alternatives, to hope.

My proposal is that our battered and endangered human habitation can also be a place of vision. The cracks in the structure threaten its collapse, let in the cold drafts, frighten us. But they can be an opportunity. We can look *through* the cracks and imagine a different possibility, we can look *at* the cracks and assess how much these remaining walls could be repaired and strengthened if they were part of the something new we can imagine. Do we need the old walls? Do we need to cut through them, make outside walls into inside ones? Or vice versa?

But what about the reason for those walls—the spaces they enclose, the spaces people actually live in? How do we live in those spaces—*can* we live in them? And—above all—with whom? We must reimagine the life in the spaces, and therefore, perhaps, drastically reimagine the nature and shape of those spaces, because the way we use the spaces determines how the walls and roofs and entrances are to be built or rebuilt. If our house is becoming uninhabitable, must we abandon it? But if we start over, how like to our old house must the new one be? It seems we must live in those spaces in very different ways.

The signs of danger and decay in the old may drive us to imagine the new, but we can only imagine something better if we understand the old, its strengths and weaknesses and the principles which underlie its building.

In the English countryside is a village called "Fawler." For centuries the name didn't appear to mean anything and nobody was bothered anyway. It was just a name. But then one day archeologists began excavating the remains of a Roman villa nearby, and uncovered a floor made of decorative tiles, of a kind common to prosperous homes in Roman Britain.

When the Angles and Saxons gradually overran Britain and the Romans or Romanized Britons of this villa fled or were killed, the incoming settlers took over the farmlands of the villa but, strangely, they did not take over the buildings that were left, or rebuild them, or even use them as foundations. The ruins were left to decay and disappear into wood and field until, centuries later, curious experts recognized the humps and bumps as signs of a long-ago settlement, and began to dig.

The Saxon settlers, it appeared, had called their own new village, *Fauflor,* from the Old English *fagflor,* meaning a colored, or painted, floor. The new settlers would not live on the "colored" floor or use it but it mattered to them, it gave them their name. Nobody knows why they did not live there. Were

they afraid of old gods who might still inhabit it and, like people living near an old minefield, need to remind themselves
where it was so as to keep away? Or was it rather a source of
good luck that they must keep untouched? Or was it simply
impractical—requiring building skills to repair that they didn't
have? We don't know the reasons but we know there was a
relationship expressed in the name—between the abandoned
buildings that reminded of a vanished way of life, and the new
structures that fitted the ways of the incomers.

It may be that the reimagining of our spaces will make it
clear that some old ones are uninhabitable for us, yet from
them we may draw identity; they are haunted, but we need to
relate to those old gods and, in our own way, learn from them
and venerate them. The use we make of physical spaces
depends on the "myth spaces" we inhabit—and whether and
how these coincide.

The particular myth explored in this book is a way to understand both the heritage and the future of the spaces in which
we choose to live, and is the myth (or the many myths) of hospitality. I shall try to show how and why hospitality is a myth
in the sense of a determining story or set of symbols that shape
the interpretation of reality and therefore decisions. But the
argument of the book is that the myth of hospitality represents
a criterion to be used in reimagining the structures of human
life that have been damaged to the point where many are no
longer habitable. To make the use of such a criterion (indeed
any criterion) possible it is first necessary to understand the
nature of human habitation, its structures, its spaces and the
relationship between spaces, and to do this at many levels of
meaning. In particular I shall be exploring throughout the star-
tling co-incidences of the way people built literal physical
structures and the way they build social, political, psychic and
spiritual structures, and how the one affects the others. The
first chapters of the book pursue this exploration of the nature
and significance of the structures we inhabit, and so allow the
actual study of the significance of hospitality as a moral and
political criterion to be developed on that basis. The deepened
awareness of the physical and metaphysical significance of

space and structure will allow me to show how the decisions made about our habitation may be affected by perceiving hospitality as a central cultural myth. I hope to show that interpretation of this myth can provide us with a valid criterion for reimagining the past so as to understand the present and make decisions about the future, showing us which of our inherited spaces offer a spiritual home and which can only be a prison. Long abandoned spaces may touch our imaginations with new possibilities; we may perceive the power of the myth to liberate us from the present and to rediscover what seemed lost.

We will bear in mind the colored floor of a buried heritage, whether or not we choose to live on it.

1

Lucien Kroll and the Translation of Spaces

*T*his chapter is about the transformation of the spaces of life
because of a transformed lifestyle, and therefore, also
about how lifestyle and life decisions transform the spaces in
which life goes on. This is relevant to the theme of hospitality
because even the most restricted sense of the word *hospitality*
has to do with the movement of people in and out of particular
spaces. Those spaces, therefore, have to be capable of accom-
modating such a flow. If they are not, either hospitality is
restricted (by restricted choices about who may be included in
it or when it may be exercised or, indeed, whether those
included will want to be there!) or else the spaces have to be
changed. The familiar, traditional and yet radical nature of such
changes will become clear. Even if we are only talking about
actual physical structures the changes involved are clearly a
matter of major spiritual and political reimagining of daily life.
But the concept of hospitality, just because it demands a
reimagining of literal physical structures, involves a transformation of the attitudes of mind, priorities, beliefs, that dictate
decisions about how to conceive of actual physical spaces. If
the requirements of hospitality have been neglected or
rejected, the restoration and the reinterpretation of its meaning
to allow decision and action require a stringent social analysis.

In order to show this we have to break through the imaginative inertia that afflicts western society. In terms of its general
social and political attitudes as reflected in the main-line media
and in the statements of public figures, no significant reimagining of the criteria for decision making is envisioned, only a

tinkering with certain areas where flexibility is perceived to be possible. In order to overcome this paralysis the method used in this book is to attempt to engage the reader in imaginative exercises that allow us freedom to perceive the world in new ways and so to allow for new possibilities.

For myself, this process of freeing the imagination in this way came about, as such things do, apparently by chance. The genesis of the images that made this book possible was like the moment when swallows, gathering for migration, seem suddenly to achieve a common decision, cease to circle and weave and greet each other and immediately set off with happy purpose in a recognized direction, though the journey ahead may be long and complex. Because this happened to me in a particular way at a particular moment it seems best simply to tell what I saw, and what it began to mean for me.

There was a program on TV, turned on idly one evening, one of a series on modern European architects called *Builders of Europe*. It concerned the work of the Belgian architect, Lucien Kroll. Kroll's work marries modern technology and industrial techniques with a wild variety of materials, spaces, inventions and surfaces to meet the spiritual as well as the practical (but for him spiritual *is* practical) needs and desires of the people who will use the buildings. The whole approach was exciting to me—neither nostalgic nor classically pure nor abstractly functional, but functional because livable and having visual references both immediately recognizable and challengingly different. The program showed how colleges, public buildings, even modular housing, could be built as structures that conveyed a sense of security, challenge and also delight.

But the thing that, for me, opened up extraordinary possibilities was the part of the program dealing with Kroll's conversions of old buildings for entirely new and different purposes.

Of the two examples shown, the first was an old stone-built farm, to be converted for the use of a religious community. This complex of beautiful, practical old buildings included a large, solid stone barn which, through centuries, had stored hay, grain and carts, and watched the comings and goings of heedless hens and pigs and busy men and women.

To turn the barn into the place of worship was an obvious idea, and not a new one. What goes on in a barn doesn't need much light, however, and a place of worship does. The obvious thing is to cut windows in the walls and so make it look much like a traditional gothic-type church; the oblong shape of a barn lends itself to this, with an altar at one end and arched windows suggesting the medieval. Thus the "barn identity" becomes only a memory. What Kroll did was to leave the walls intact but knock a big hole in one slope of the roof, letting in light onto an altar placed not at one end but against the wall on the opposite side. And, having made the hole, he did not then put in skylight windows, but filled the jagged space with glass tiles instead. The result was that the lines and identity of the barn were preserved, but the hole torn in the roof, the light pouring in, indicated a change, a new beginning. There was a double vision of the old identity and the new one, never coinciding, yet present in the same space. The purposes and meanings of the past were not mere memory but still there, to be apprehended in the present, while the new use, and the means to it, established themselves without compromise or nostalgia. Kroll had reimagined the new use of the space out of an awareness of the old one.

Another conversion was even more dramatic. Three Victorian terrace houses—large, solid and brick-built—were to become the home of a school of drama and dance. The old houses were originally designed to provide appropriately spacious and dignified rooms for comfortable, respectable middle-class families with servants and lots of furniture. The rooms were large but rigid, symmetrical, each house identical, for people whose lives were as regular as their incomes. A drama school, on the other hand, needs large and adaptable spaces for practice and rehearsal, it needs classrooms, library, study spaces, above all it must allow for quick moves from one occupation to another. Strikingly other than the purpose of the old houses, a drama school is of its nature changeable, as new people and new ideas come and work and interact and leave.

All this naturally required a great deal of knocking down of walls, redesigning access systems, realigning of entrances. Kroll did all these things, and succeeded in turning three houses into one school, but he did it in such a way that the original three houses continued to be imaginatively and structurally "present." For instance, ceilings and walls had been breached to provide a huge practice room, and from it open-tread stairs ran up alongside the exposed brick of the remaining massive interior load-bearing wall, which had once been the partition between two of the houses. And from this upper floor, from what had been the next-door house, one could see a library, through the wall between the two old houses where a gaping hole in the massive brickwork allowed both vision and passage. No doorway, no neatly framed vista taking the eye directly to the library gallery beyond and the great room below, but just a hole of ragged brick, arresting the eye momentarily with the awareness of the nature of the old dividing wall, still at work, still supporting the building and its new role. You would have to walk through that hole to follow the neatly carpeted way into the sparsely and elegantly functional spaces beyond. So every time people in the drama school go through that hole they will have to be conscious, if only subliminally, of the sturdy brickwork of long ago, still firmly and courageously facilitating the life and work of a very different time. In this reimagined building, neither old nor new detract from each other; both are present but distinct and mutually respectful.

It is possible for a photographer with certain kinds of lenses to present objects at different distances with equal clarity and distinctness. A painter can focus on landscape beyond as well as on figures in a foreground, and paint each in as much detail as he or she likes. The unaided human eye cannot do this. If I want to admire a rose in my garden I allow the landscape beyond to recede into a background of green haze, but if I look over my garden wall at the view of moor and woodland the branches of the sycamore that frame the distant scene become blurry and irrelevant. I cannot focus on both at once, I cannot be equally visually conscious of near and far in the same moment, yet when I think about them they are both part of my awareness of the place where I stand. When Lucien Kroll changes the purposes of an old building the nature of human vision, both literal and symbolic, is not altered as it can be by a painter or a camera. The spectator—and especially the spectator who is also the dweller in the changed structure—is not *simultaneously conscious* of past and present, though both are, in their constructs, simultaneously there and interacting. One can be consciously aware of—literally focused on—the structures enduring from old usage, or one can be consciously aware of new organization of space, new purposes and possibilities. Yet while one focuses on the one, the other is there, out of focus both visually and intellectually, but visibly and importantly *there.*

This shifting vision becomes a routine part of daily and ordinary perception. It can shift awareness toward a habit of linking continuity and change, a link which, most of the time, isn't consciously considered, but is simply part of the language of perception. Developing a conscious double awareness can develop a capacity for decision making that is founded in material reality and long-term human experience to a much greater extent than is the case when past and present (and therefore future) are separate imaginative categories with only deliberate and temporary connections, created for specific purposes and not arising from ongoing habits of perception and verification.

A good example of a way of thinking that quite normally deals with this "double awareness" is that of Australian Aboriginal people. Dr. Helen Verran, who teaches at the University of Melbourne and was adopted into an Aboriginal clan in Arnhemland, has written (in her book *Singing the Land*) and lectured about the Aboriginal way of drawing together past, present and future in the establishment of belonging in an area of land—but the Aboriginal people would not call it an "area" since they do not "measure" land but live in it as a home. It is necessary for them frequently and routinely to create and re-create their land by rituals of dancing and singing, in which ancestors and descendants are equally present. The "location" of the ceremony, however, is not the place where an observer would perceive it to be happening, but by imagination, and therefore, in reality it happens throughout all the interwoven ways of that vast landscape which is home. It is difficult for a western person to enter into this imaginatively, but developing something equivalent to this "presence" of past and present, near and far, in one method of perception is essential if we are to achieve imaginative flexibility in responding to the needs of our time, and it was Lucien Kroll's architectural adaptations—to use a rather tame word for a revolutionary concept—that opened up for me a way to understand this as something that could make sense to people using western imaginative categories.

These new imaginative categories can reveal a way to think and act. They provide a language of perception which, in turn, prompts the attempt to work out their applicability to the massive issues of continuity and change in so many aspects of living. In all of these areas we can learn to use new "tools" of perception in ways that are manageable and immediate, in contexts that are familiar. The image of a building, a structure, has to be usable in practical ways that enable us to have confidence in it, and we also have to use it in order to become accustomed to recognizing how the most immediate spaces of our lives—personal and spiritual, family and home, neighborhood, work—are related to what appear to be more "impersonal" structures—political and ecclesial, cultural, economic and scientific. We need to learn to use the image of structure with ease and accuracy, through areas of experience, exploring the "house" of our lives in various ways. One discovery uncovers another, like the excavation of an ancient city. This way of thinking about the mutual influences of structural spaces and lives will make it possible to explore, later on, the need for a recognizable criterion for making decisions about the building or adaptation of structures, whether literal or mythical. A few reflections on the complexities of this way of thinking and perceiving may be helpful (or may just complicate things).

First, the experience of "shifting vision" encountered in Kroll's conversions of old buildings to new purposes is in fact the exploitation of anachronism. That is, there is the juxtaposition of two or more "times" in one "time" ("chronos") through the coincidence of their concrete and visible artifacts. For instance, it is "anachronistic" for a Victorian family's careful separation of servants and "gentry," and of one household from another, to be used to breach those very categories and provide a setting in which life and activity flow unchecked between houses and categories. The new categories and distinctions (pupils and teachers and administrators) contradict and even invert the class categories reflected in the old building. (Servants are paid by the "masters" and serve them, and do what they are told. Pupils pay—or are paid for—to be taught, but obey those who are paid!) The awareness of these anachronisms is essential to the shifting vision that gives a sense of energy and possibility. The time ("chronos") element, of old and new, with precise dates, is contradicted and in a sense wiped out: "ana." This produces a kind of imaginative shock, as if the solid floor had given way. It is in these "gaps," when normal ways of thinking and perceiving suddenly fail, that another kind of vision becomes possible. These are the moments of creation, of mystical perception, those drastic breaks with normal perception that allow scientific or artistic breakthrough. The biographies of scientists, for instance, record over and over again that the moments of discovery occurred when the process of study, experiment, deduction, had broken down, and in the "gap" intuition allowed a wholly unexpected conjunction of ideas to emerge. This isn't just haphazard, or an excuse to avoid drudgery; intense logical study and thought goes on and *then,* when it can go no further, the structure breaks down and something "other" can be perceived. You can't have an "anachronism" without a "chronos" that is accepted and understood, which is why enlightenment through drugs or similar mind-changes doesn't work. So the basis of genuine and usable newness is the intelligent awareness of the possibility revealed in anachronism. The "chronos" awareness gives an element of visual, imaginable stability and conceptual continuity from which the mind can begin. This stability paradoxically makes possible the spiritual and intellectual risk-taking that is required if real and valid change is to happen.

Another example of the use of anachronism is the Christian theological concept of sacrament. Sacramental practice deals with the physical reality of material things—bread and wine of eucharist, water of baptism, human sexuality in marriage—and proposes each of them as a privileged locus of encounter with the intangible "reality" of spiritual power and divine grace. Neither reality is allowed to swallow up the other. The material thing retains its physical characteristics, yet something else is fully at work in it. The eucharistic concept is particularly powerful because (without going into various metaphysically specific explanations offered by different Christian traditions) it postulates the undiluted reality of the saving presence of Christ to the believer in the material reality of bread and wine. However this may be interpreted (as simple memorial, as symbol, as exchange of substance in Aristotelian categories) there is a powerful anachronism at work when two normally distinct categories of thought are forced together. The "chronos" of Christ and the "chronos" of the believer are broken down by the action of memory and symbol (however "symbol" be understood) and a "gap" is created within which power is released and faith becomes possible. The anachronistic power of symbol is also inherent in the power of language, which consists of symbols. (It is not coincidental that the old word for Christian creeds is "symbol.")

The second consideration that seems helpful is that the idea of a house in bad condition as a place of opportunity suggests making use of the accidental and unforeseen collapse of elements of the building, creating gaps. So far I have talked mostly about examples of the deliberate creation of holes and gaps for foreseen purposes, but the two experiences are related in various ways. If part of a structure breaks down it is often because it has been neglected or misused and any damage has been unnoticed or not considered important. This indicates already that the weakened part of the structure is not being used as it was intended to be used, with full deliberation and understanding. If so, it probably needs to be altered or perhaps removed and replaced. The act of becoming aware that the thing is damaged forces questions about how the space has been used, why—or if—it is still needed, and its relation to the whole building. Does neglect of this part indicate a need for more radical changes in the use of the whole? If so, what kind of changes?

In other words, the presence of damage through neglect or misuse (or even, all too possibly, by deliberate intent in war, rebellion or riot) creates either actual "holes" or cracks, or indicates that changes are needed involving perhaps more than repair. Deliberate "holes" will have to be made to make the area usable in different ways, and may well indicate rethinking of the use and organization of other spaces related to the part where there is obvious damage.

As an illustration and example we can think of this in terms of educational structure. When pupils leave school unable to read, and when there is a high drop-out rate, it becomes clear that something in the scholastic structure is not working. The obvious place where damage is visible is in the classroom. It is (in many cases literally) "leaking." Good education is not going on there, and the first reaction is to try to repair the visible damage by demanding such changes as higher qualifications for teachers, more emphasis on "basics" in early school years, enforcement of dress codes, more involvement of parents. But if such measures do not work, or only partly work, more questions are raised. Is it possible that the damage to the "classroom" part of the educational structure is due not so much to misuse or neglect by teachers and pupils as to inappropriate pressures on the classroom by the whole educational structure? Maybe those demands are too great for classrooms already trying to deal with stresses and challenges of contemporary culture for which they were not designed? Taking a step away to obtain a better vantage point, we can further ask if the whole educational structure is itself reacting to false expectations and values placed on it by the society? If so, do we need to redesign (or remove?) the whole "classroom" concept? Do we need to rethink the entire educational structure in response to educational needs differently conceived? If we think in this way, what we are doing is similar to what Kroll did with the Victorian terrace houses where there may well have been damage due to neglect of no-longer-functional kitchens, or of attic bedrooms left empty because now regarded as uninhabitable by a generation that can no longer believe that servants don't feel the cold.

Learning to perceive change in a new way means seeing visions of possibility through accidentally created cracks and holes, as well as—or leading to—the envisioning of change by creating holes where none were before. And in either case the nature of the structure has to be understood, so that we know where holes can exist or be made without bringing down the entire building.

This has to do with the basic continuity of "architectural" principles—really "engineering" principles—that apply to social and political engineering as much as to buildings. These are by no means independent of one another.

The third reflection arises from the second, and it concerns the way—vital to the argument and conclusion of this book—in which architecture does act as a kind of indicator of cultural assumptions and priorities: architects design structures that house not only people but the myths by which we live. We can tell from how people build what they think about humans and their needs, about cultural priorities, about relations between classes and sexes and races. When houses can be described, in Le Corbusier's famous phrase, as "machines for living," and high-rise buildings are designed like storage units for industrial workers in their non-working hours, the underlying social principles are obvious. Le Corbusier (spiritual child of Newton and Descartes, worshiper of a God who wound up the perfect machine and ruled detachedly over a clockwork universe) also wrote glowingly of the beauty of American grain silos, standing up in the great plains like modern "cathedrals." But the silos were in fact potent symbols of the ruin of the small farmer as land was increasingly concentrated in the vast commercial farms, and led ultimately to the erosion of the shallow soil when the prairies were plowed up to grow huge quantities of grain, producing the "dust-bowl," as the soil blew away.

To build, or rebuild, anything successfully, whether it be a home, a family, a church, a culture, a language, a business or a nation, you have to understand the principles that allow such a structure to stand at all. Sometimes, for instance, medieval architects got it wrong. They added a grandiose spire to a church tower and the whole thing fell in. They miscalculated the effect of the thrust of a new roof on a building adequate to the old one and the walls cracked. So they learned—not to avoid challenging new projects but to understand better the underlying principles that would make them possible. But the builders of the great cathedrals were not only creators of innovative building techniques, they built out of shared myths, a coherent philosophy of living, a strong sense of the human vocation and human spiritual symbolic needs, which translated into an awareness of what kinds of spaces made possible effective ritual and good acoustics. They built chantries where mass could be offered for the souls of members of wealthy families (the myth accommodated an acceptance of the ability of wealth to obtain advantages after as well as before death) and made grandiose shrines for the holy relics whose material reality linked earth-bound humans with those humans who had achieved heaven and whose heavenly power was still potent in their bones. They designed spaces to allow the pilgrims who came seeking those relics and their possibilities of marvelous healing, and who brought much needed offerings, to circulate easily. These spaces also reflected, later in the middle ages, the clericalism and spiritual dualism of their culture, shutting off the laity from the sacred spaces of choir and high altar. In all this vast energy of architectural creation the builders reflected, in fact, the religious feeling and assumptions of their times, but at many levels. They built for people what people wanted and responded to.

In terms of houses, the very poor of the middle ages in Europe were indeed squalidly housed, in whatever spaces could be found, but those who owned or rented a little land could build to their own needs, within the limits of their income, available technology and cultural imagination. Then again, when the early settlers came to the new world, the dwellings of ordinary people were built according to traditional European designs that were fitted to the pockets and needs of the occupants, and changed as needs changed, reflecting the different uses of space as trades became more specialized.

Many homes in medieval towns, and in those of the "new world" at first, were indeed cramped and unsanitary because the inhabitants could not afford better, had little idea of hygiene and had to fit their dwellings inside defensive city walls or defensive wooden stockades and with minimum space per household. It was not until the late eighteenth century that the flight from the villages to the cities was caused by the creation of new industries and their factories and the loss of rural industry, and homes were built in huge numbers to accommodate workers and their families as cheaply as possible.

Cottages had previously been built for farm laborers and others by landowners, and their quality depended on how a landowner valued his workers, but mass-produced housing began with the industrial revolution, when housing was created to suit the needs of the mine or factory owners of the new industrial age, not of the occupants. The straight rows of identical terraces of houses, the narrow streets and narrower back alleys, or back-to-back houses without alleys at all, and the lack of communal facilities, show clearly enough the priorities of the builders. To build homes as near the factories as possible, for as little as possible, was the requirement. Workers were "hands," and as such need not be consulted. They would live in these houses because they had no choice: they needed the jobs to stay alive.

At the same time that these squalid streets were being built for the "hands," the mansions of the factory or mine owners, built in gothic baronial or elegant classical style, proclaimed that they regarded themselves as different and separate. They housed their servants in the attics and basements, out of sight except when providing services that required at least minimum visibility, such as waiting at table. The servants' quarters, like the factory workers' cottages, were an architectural indication of the social value placed on the occupants. Even now, the mansions of mine owners in Appalachia—in Spanish or Colonial style—indicate a total rejection of kinship with the miners living in wooden shacks without running water. On the positive side, and as a reaction to all this, men such as Josiah

Salt built "Saltaire" near Bradford in Yorkshire to show that good housing for factory workers, bath houses, recreational facilities (non-alcoholic) and parks were good business as well as good religion, and social reformers of the Anglo-Catholic revival deliberately built large gothic churches in the industrial cities because, to them, such buildings were a statement that the poorest had a right to a sacred space of beauty and dignity.

The assumptions of our own time about human nature and human needs is made very clear by the presence in virtually every major city in the world of those high-rise blocks that accommodate the largest possible number of people on the smallest amount of land, without any common spaces or normal means of meeting one another except in concrete alleys or on balconies. Similarly, school buildings that look like factories display a definite philosophy of education, and prisons designed to look like medieval fortresses are eloquent of attitudes to those who offend against power. And people bring in plants and pictures to their little air-conditioned office cubicles in an attempt to humanize working days in places where no windows open and many rooms have no windows anyway.

There is really no need to dot the *i*s and cross the *t*s. The struggles of many architects to find better ways are themselves a confession of the social sin that other architects, with those who commission such places, have committed. But architects and designers and those who engage them are themselves in turn the victims of the same cultural assumptions that expect that the majority—whether as householders or workers or students or criminals—should be accommodated according to the views and for the convenience of those who hold power. And all of them learn (that is how education is designed) to accept the categories and descriptions that are assigned to them. They may try to rebel, but usually they don't have much success since they lack alternative imaginative categories with which to describe their discontent or organize a different vision of the future.

If architecture is a good cultural indicator, then that also makes clear the extent to which solid, visible things such as buildings are inextricably linked to apparently invisible things such as health and choice and freedom and friendship and hope, or their opposites. If a builder puts too heavy a roof on a house and it collapses, then it is clear that he or she has not understood the basic principles of building, but if we overstrain the fabric of social life or personal spiritual growth or if we wrench language for ideological purposes, these structures also give way and cease to be useful. There is such a thing as "language fatigue," analogous to "mental fatigue." Ideological overstress eventually destroys sensitivity to the words; even "bad" language has to get more and more obscene to cause the shock that is its purpose: eventually it loses its power and becomes "outdated." In political rhetoric, concepts like "family values" and "back to basics" are at first effective rallying cries for people frightened and fed up with growing poverty and crime, but eventually they produce only cynicism. So if we are to undertake the business of change we need to be aware of the entire human fabric as interrelated, and language will inevitably prove to be the means of discovering and working with (rather than against) that interrelatedness.

Finally, in order to perceive the possibility of making creative holes, or creatively using holes that "happen," we have to let go a lot of perfectionism. We have to recognize that when human life is full of energy and vitality it is also very messy. Perfect good taste is only possible in spaces where rules are rigid and the servants are out of sight, whether in the basements and attics, or in a third world barrio, or in a factory or sweat-shop in one of our own cities.

Perhaps the best symbol of this energetic disorder-in-order is a market of the traditional kind in Europe or Mexico or other places where people come together to sell all kinds of things to all kinds of other people in a space assigned for the purpose. Such a coming together of traders and buyers has to be organized and have some basic rules if it is to work, but the attraction of markets (and where there is a place specifically designated for them it allows for this) is their exuberant variety, the bustle and noise and jostling, the chance of finding a treasure for not much, the jokes and bargaining. People go to a market to buy and sell, they hope to make some prudent purchases or a good profit, but buyers also go for the fun and companionship. Markets are often places for street shows, for displays of art, for music and conjuring tricks and political speeches, for soliciting donations for charity and handing out tracts about the end of the world. A market is also an attractive place for pickpockets and prostitutes and drug dealers. At the end of the day the mess left behind takes a while to clean up, and street people pick through the remains in the hope of a sandwich or a dropped jacket or a cigarette.

A market is a structure, or rather it is a complex of many structures interacting—physical, economic and social structures. It is quite fragile. It may become too crime-ridden, so people won't come. To prevent crime it may become too regimented, and soon people aren't interested. It may offer so much highly colored trash and so much loud music that it becomes mostly a fun fair, or it may become so utilitarian that it isn't fun. The mix is important, and delicate. It allows for bad taste as well as good, for practicality and fantasy, for legal profit and a little illegal profit as well. The "structure" of a market, in fact, turns out not to be something that can be described in terms of the regulations that are applied to it or of the space in which it is located. It is more easily understood in terms of "chaos theory." For a long time scientists did not try to describe such systems as clouds or flowing water because they didn't fit any of the available categories. But study has shown that these "chaotic" systems do have a structure, a kind of inherent order that cannot be precisely predicted or directed but which is observable using computer technology. Human organizations, as we are discovering, are often better understood in such a way than by trying to make them fit criteria developed to judge machines.

This image of human interaction provides a reference point when we are trying to understand the way in which structures may change and yet have a continuity and a humanness, may even appear "chaotic" and yet have purpose and direction. We may not look for what we like to think of as "perfection" (which is essentially controllable); we must look for what allows life to flourish. Like "Cadet Roussel" in the French folk song we may find we have roofless houses *qui n'ont ni poutres ni chevrons,* but instead of pulling them down we can, like this eccentric landlord, decide that at least they can be "pour loger les hirondelles." Swallows, after all, need places to live, and instead of assuming that swallows need structures without roof beams or trusses, perhaps we can learn to create spaces that are hospitable to both swallows and humans.

2

Can We Live in This House?

With the questions raised—some at least—and some tools of perception identified, the next step is in a sense to go back to the beginning and raise the same questions, but now to do so using the image of the house, the structure of life, as a way to define the nature of the griefs we endure, the fears we entertain, the possibilities we may open up. In order to perceive the opening up of possibilities we have to acknowledge fully the destruction that has done the opening. Can we live in this house?

Inevitably, though depressingly because of its subject, this chapter is mostly about what is wrong with the human habitation and how and why, and it may also seem all too obvious. But it seemed important to pursue the what and how of our predicament in terms of the structural image.

Detectives (in books at least) are no longer shown, like Sherlock Holmes, moving step by step through a flawless process of deduction to an inevitable conclusion. They proceed by a mixture of reason, intuition, teamwork and luck. (Even Holmes relied more on luck than he might have been willing to admit.) One bit of evidence casts light on something that happened before, which at the time seemed to have no special significance. A connection is perceived between events that at first seemed disconnected.

We must, then, revisit the scene of the crime, which is not an unjust way to describe what is happening to our world, and to look at the place with eyes retrained by the use of the image of the house (structure, building, *home*) of our lives.

It doesn't matter what label you attach to the building. You can call it culture or church or language or family or education or democracy or a number of other possible names; they merely indicate the focus of particular concern that we feel as we are driven to admit that the structure is dangerously damaged. That is, it isn't doing what it was meant to do, it isn't predictable and solid, it is no longer—as we would like it to be—something you can take for granted and not even think about because it is simply there. It can't be lived in with any degree of comfort or even safety—yet there may not be anywhere else to live.

Looking back, it can seem that once upon a time the only problem was learning to live in the building in the appropriate way, and the only problem people were the ones who didn't know how to do that, at least to an acceptable degree. And it was possible to measure the acceptability of people, including oneself, but how well they learned to live in "it" (whatever "it" is). People fell between the extremes of, at one end, those whom one revered as preservers and even architects of structure—the geniuses, the saints, the sages and patriarchs—and at the other end those who continually failed to live in it—the "black sheep" in the family, heretics in the church, truants in school, rebels, and eccentrics in society, criminals or anarchists in the state (and, in language, people who swore or mixed their metaphors or split their infinitives) as well as those who evaded responsibility or even rejected it, to whom the building was either an enemy or an irrelevance. Yet philosopher Kathryn Addelson in her book *Moral Passages* has pointed out that these "hardened offenders," the people who refuse to use a space as they have been told it must be used, those who insist on looking out when they should look in, and in when they should look out, being upstairs when they should be down, and intruding into spaces that are "out of bounds" or not officially "there," may be the geniuses as well as the criminals (it depends how you define either one), the saints as well as the heretics, the pioneers as well as the rebels.

These "misfits" only survived, if they did, because there were some inhabitants (social workers, nurses, missionaries, for instance) who respected the ways of the house to the point of taking responsibility for integrating, in some marginal way, those who didn't appear to fit. It was always a moot point whether they tried to do this for the sake of the misfits or for the sake of the structure.

So it seems that at this time we have to practice a kind of inversion of the ways we have been taught to think about the inhabitants of the building, because we now realize that the description (hero or heretic, saint or sinner) depends on who shapes the language. The dominant culture has decided who is acceptable within the structure it created and has named the categories of acceptability or otherwise to fit its ordering. The dominant culture, then, decided how to deal with the "misfits," and if they were not to be simply eliminated (a fairly frequent choice), then categories were found and ways devised to include them without allowing them to challenge the official description.

It seems to me that the way any society categorizes its "misfits" and how it accommodates them is a very important indication of the moral health of that society. The issue here is that, from the modern vantage point, we have tended to assume that the descriptions of levels of acceptability passed on to us by past societies can be taken at face value. That these descriptions are now being questioned indicates that more people are willing to experiment with the inversion of categories and even to rewrite history. Needless to say, there is a lot of panic resistance to this, because it undermines the sense of historical continuity. We are back to the cracks in the structure, the need for shifting vision.

Of course in reality the building was never as solid as those who wrote popular history suggested. The building was always falling down and being patched and altered and rebuilt. From the time of Socrates, and no doubt before, the older generation has complained that the young have no respect for old ways, and threaten the fabric of society. But within any given culture the falling down and rebuilding generally happened very slowly, except in the case of a major catastrophe like the black death or an invasion of the Huns. And although the additions and subtractions of the past were visible to later generations, they had been there so long that they too were felt to be simply there, part of the inherited and secure whole.

One reason why continuity can seem more real than change has been that those negatively affected by change were, or became, historically marginal. They became, often, the "misfits" who had to be categorized out of significant existence. When, for instance, peasants in England were dispossessed by enclosure of land for sheep they had no vote and no political voice; the change benefited the landowners who interpreted it as part of their immemorial right to the land. When indigenous "Bushmen" in Africa are driven off their ancient lands by farmers or mineral prospectors, they are equally invisible to those who write history in terms of the development of what they perceive as "empty" land. Changes of which we inherited the results seldom seemed to threaten the structure as a whole, because the real continuity was that described by the people in power, the ones who designed the structure. When changes actually did threaten the whole structure most people were quite unprepared. The French revolution, for instance, came as a total surprise to people who expected the old regime to continue forever, though perhaps with improvements. They had chosen not to notice the misery of the poor but also not to notice the increasing discontent of a rising professional middle class that had education and money and did not choose to be ruled by aristocratic fiat. The same could be said of the Russian version, and in both cases the actual structures of class and oppression that provoked the revolution were later reinstalled under different names. The house, in other words, was rebuilt on the same pattern with new stylistic details.

The variety of inherited styles from the past has actually increased some of the false sense of security we inherited because it proved that the thing could and would continue, since it had survived so much. European cathedrals admirably display this process of successful patching and adaptation over centuries. The English ones, though damaged, even survived Cromwell's military iconoclasm, and the French ones survived the revolution.

Old words can change meanings, but still carry their original flavors. Old models of family may be "improved" and adapted, becoming kinder and "fairer" (for instance, in many countries an abused woman can now get a divorce) but remain basically the same. Old ways of worship, with the symbols embedded in them (hand washing during the Catholic mass, for instance, and peculiar garments) may lose their original practical significance but acquire symbolic ones, at least for a while. The language of theology hardens like old oak beams; the hooks in them were once for hanging hams or strings of onions and now may display bunches of dried flowers. Old ways of scholarship became ways of assessing social standing, as a minimal knowledge of Latin and Greek was, for a long time, the mark of a gentleman long after those languages ceased to be in use as everyday communication among scholars. The real question in education became how to preserve the social structure by teaching different classes of people differently, while not admitting (except in South Africa until recently) that that was the purpose. Shakespeare is still upsetting people, still oppressing children and exciting them, and suddenly discovered to be material for films. Mozart, too.

As long as the pace of the damage was slow and the patching and changing only perceptible to those with no voice to point it out, the sense of security could be passed on in terms of history, destiny, the natural law, the God-given roles in society. Even when quite large bits of wall fell down it wasn't disturbing because clever people were busy rebuilding it, and perhaps including a new door leading to a new room, which increased the comfort and convenience of the whole. If it became impossible to accept exactly seven days of creation, it was then possible to walk through into a new room called evolution, which reinforced man's sense of self-importance and provided attractive vistas for enlightened appreciation of less developed creatures. If women fought for the vote and broke down some areas of social expectation, the result was that in the newly opened space a large work force of women could be accommodated, sufficiently educated to do teaching and clerical jobs but not needing to be paid as much as men. Changes in the building were sometimes worrying, but they did not disturb the basic assumption that the thing would endure as the structure of being. It had to because beyond it, it was tacitly understood, could only be savagery and madness.

But all this certainty has crumbled. In all the areas of living that make up the house of our lives the pace of destruction has quickened to the point where the sense of continuity is threatened or lost. The reason is not only the cataclysmic quality of twentieth century events. Huge disasters and violent changes, man-made and "natural," have happened before, from the collapse of the Roman empire to the industrial revolution via the black death, the religious wars of the seventeenth century, the exploitation of the "new world" and the colonization of Africa and large parts of Asia. But, until recently, awareness of the significance of such events spread only slowly beyond those directly affected. In earlier centuries a lack of historical perspective in largely illiterate and localized cultures made unlikely the kinds of analysis that could challenge the continuity of accepted religious and political views. The changes were happening, but people had their noses right up against them. There was no space to perceive how even huge changes could actually make irreparable holes in the fabric of life-structuring assumptions.

So it has been not merely the scale of destruction that has rendered impossible the belief in inherent continuity in the structure of western culture. Decisive, rather, has been the speed of communication, not only of news of events themselves but of reflection on them and question and doubt. What might once have been disturbing exchanges between a few academic gentlemen, perhaps conveyed (if one had good enough connections) to like-minded others through the decent delays of print, is now tossed around the world by internet, or radio or television—unedited, speculative, unauthorized and immediate. Minds are attacked with experiences in picture and word, image and interpretation, facts selected for their shock value plus available panic comment, all of them assaulting existing assumptions and expectations at a speed that allows little time for identification of the damage, still less for repair.

In the last thirty years or so, the pace of destruction has outstripped the ability easily to perceive continuity. The building was in danger of falling down, and nobody anymore could take it for granted that repair was desirable, even if possible. After all, the first step in building, however modest the project, is imagination, and the imagination of this generation of western culture is to a great extent taken over by the images of change: newness, especially new destruction, is more arresting, more preoccupying and therefore more saleable than images of continuity.

One important exception to this is in the area of nostalgic tourism, the Disney World syndrome, where the traditional, the craft-made, the "timeless" and the "historic" are to be discovered, preserved or re-created precisely as an antidote, an escape from the experienced loss of real continuity and tradition. But neither the vivid images of inevitable and drastic change nor the artificial images of lost continuity allow imagination the space or the tools to consider the plight of the damaged building as a fact, an experience, a place to end and to begin. Damaged—even badly damaged—does not mean ruined. The house of our common life is not an archaeological survival, but neither is it a building in which anyone can live fully with a sense of hope and opportunity.

I am talking of the structures of our lives—political, religious, cultural, linguistic and domestic. Great holes have been punched in them, revealing unexplored and scary spaces. There are a third as many single parent families in the U.S.A. as those with two parents, and the proportion is evening up. Some children have two parents of the same sex. Many people go to church but more or less easily ignore aspects of religion and morals they find unrealistic or incredible. The democratic structures being (at least for a time) vociferously claimed in eastern Europe or Africa are a dirty or irrelevant game to many in the west. Education based on enlightenment principles of individualism and competition runs off the indifferent shoulders of the poor, white or black, who know that in "competition" they will lose (because the values are written that way) and who don't buy the myth of "timeless culture" when their own time is only a cage.

The accumulation of this kind of experience (the steady crumbling of the roof of protective certainties, leaving gaps through which the winds of fear whistle eerily, the worm of doubt in the beams, the fungus sprouting from carefully painted walls) has led to understandably violent reactions of various kinds.

One is the fundamentalist reaction that affirms that the structures of society, religious and secular, have but one right and eternal form, and if they have been damaged by the forces of evil they must be mended and rebuilt in exactly the same way as before. The problem with this essentially a-historical reaction is that the psycho-social materials that built the structures of the past are no longer available. They have been too much weakened by a scientific (or at least pseudo-scientific) world-view. The traditional kinds of faith and morality were as much a social expectation as traditional gender and class distinctions and have lost their inevitability along with the political categories they reflected and reinforced. What was once acceptable because "everyone" accepted it now has to be asserted on faith in the face of questioning; what could once be taken for granted as the belief and practice of "right thinking" people must be urged as the possession of exclusive spiritual enlightenment. Moral blackmail and promises of exclusive reward for the faithful are used to rebuild the fallen walls and roof, but these are fragile materials needing constant reinforcement, and although the results give an appearance of traditional strength and reassuring consistency, they can collapse with the ludicrous and pathetic speed of the Bakker gospel empire.

But, as I suggested, we are now faced with the realization that the structures of living always have been in a state of constant disintegration and repair and that the repair changes the character of the building. This realization is one that has only become possible in a time and a culture that has a long historical perspective but also a wide geographic and ethnographic one. At this point in history we are able to perceive how different cultures, arising in different climates and conditions of life, develop ways of living, speaking, thinking and relating that are so different from each other that communication between them, though creating links, can also be deeply misleading and alienating.

An example of this is the attempt by some anthropologists to understand the power of certain African or Caribbean spiritual teachers—the healing, the curses, the ecstasies and the attitudes to life. The deliberately non-judgmental stance of western scientists toward phenomena that would once have been rejected as fraudulent or condemned as evil, the choice to distance themselves from past attitudes of superiority, is intended to be respectful but ends up being demeaning because there is no common awareness of the phenomena, they are still things to be observed, not shared, and the observation is itself an alienating act. The two cultures cannot assume a common language of perception. The very experience in each culture of everyday objects and acts, and of natural phenomena, is so different in significance and "weight" that no real "translation" seems possible. The options can seem to be an agreed uncomprehending politeness or the domination of one over the other.

This kind of experience can make it seem that the structure of living constitutes not so much a building as an ever changing illusion, one that each human community creates by consent in order to survive, and this hypothesis is one that appeals to people caught in the nets of ambiguity as they try to understand choices. The building's appearance of solidity and permanence is, in this view, at any given moment the result of a tacit collusion. If this is so, the only honest attitude is one that simply acknowledges the usefulness of the illusory structure, always aware that it has no final reality. This implies that all statements of fact, even the most "scientific," are necessarily context-dependent because the words and concepts used to make the statement are themselves in process of change even as they are spoken or written. In fact the act of using concepts is in itself a disintegrating act, for every utterance of a word exposes it to the influences of the moment and the place, energies it has never before encountered. (The block on valid imagination that this perception creates can, however, be

understood in another way, and the next chapter explores this.)
• This contextualizing of all human cultural exchange is the opposite extreme to the frantic assertion of a fundamental and unchangeable basis for living. In between the two are many degrees and kinds of adaptations to the fear of chaos. Some are positive and adventurous. There are attempts both exciting and frightening to take advantage of the collapse of parts of the structure, claiming freedom to try out entirely new ways of speaking, relating, creating, just as in Britain the Saxon villagers chose to build in their own way, without regard to the ruined structures of their Roman predecessors. But, like those Saxons, those who build new spaces find themselves relating to the old whether they like it or not, even using old names or descriptions. The public making of alternative sexual choices is one such attempt, and it relates to traditional kinds of sexual behavior in similar ways, moving suspiciously around the word *family,* not sure what to do with "love" but wanting it, and seeking in new ways the comfort and stability that many of us were taught to perceive in the old structures.

In the arts in the nineteenth century the impressionist awareness of new possibilities of capturing qualities of light made a modest hole in previously defined artistic space, and through it could be perceived the aesthetic challenges of producing quasi "accidental" combinations of color and form. Out of this emerged the metaphysical/tactile experimentation with the aesthetic relationship between surface, symbol and form, with the line between painting and sculpture breaking down. Connected with this are the aesthetics of encounter (explored long ago in Arthur Koestler's book *The Act of Creation*), the deliberate yet uncontrollable exploitation of the coincidence of incompatibles. Barriers between media, between aesthetic categories, between art and non-art, collapsed in a cloud of dust, allowing people to explore the sources of aesthetics in the interface of personal history, cultural moment, symbolic power and available materials both mental and physical. It was all very confusing, and great fun, as well as opening up depths of revelation in the spaces smashed open. It was risk and fury and vision.

The greatest movement to take advantage of breaks in the structure and make a few more is—not surprisingly—the women's movement. The perceived gaps were originally modest. Early feminism took advantage of the contradictions in patriarchal attitudes to women who were expected, for instance, in one class to do the bulk of the world's labor and in another to be incapable of exertion, and used the contradiction to break open a large space, consistent still with the accepted feminine roles. Nursing, "good works," and teaching could be understood as extensions of the womanly role in the home. When women did achieve the right to operate professionally in these "womanly" spheres, and to that extent breached the walls of the domestic spaces, larger vistas perceived through these holes prompted some further energetic smashing of patriarchal structures. This was made easier by the obvious need for women's services in the growth of business and industry, and especially by their proven ability to take over male roles in time of war. Severe limits are still experienced by women in political and economic life, and the continuing underlying contempt for women persists, evidenced, for instance, in continued widespread condoning of domestic abuse in practice if not in law. Structures that betray an obvious flimsiness can still operate to perpetuate oppressive attitudes because they are part of perceptions by both sexes which, though certainly not unquestioned, are still present and workable. This applies also in matters of racism and other divisions based on systems that (however unjust) once made political and economic sense in terms of the prevailing ideology, but survive through the pressure of unacknowledged fear of loss of security if the system should collapse.

There are darker ways in which the disintegration of the inherited building releases demonic power, because of the great fear of the loss of secure support for one's life. The huge and convincing power of Nazism arose to replace the shattered walls of German self-respect with something stronger—something appealing to the power of ancient myths and of the newer myths of science. Its success was built on the fact that it is "myth spaces"—our spiritually-needed interpretation of the "shape" of history and culture—that enable us to *see* our present reality in a way that fits our needs. Nazism built fast and impressively on those myth-foundations, and it *did* impress most people at the time; it swept away for the purpose anything that might raise doubts about the myth, anything that reminded of another way, another culture. The same ideology serves the same purpose in many countries as the century nears its end, appealing, for instance, to people afraid of losing racial distinction when they have nothing much else to distinguish them. As in South Africa for generations, so now in cities of the United States and Europe, "the myth spaces" formed by hatred are available to give shape to fallen walls through which may be glimpsed terrifying visions of disintegration of identity.

A phenomenon noticed by a number of therapists is the growth of incidents of ritual sexual abuse of children, and the accumulating evidence of the prevalence of Satanic cults of varying degrees of seriousness, from the ludicrous and amateurish to the powerful, well organized and well endowed. The secrecy is part of the power, providing members with a strong sense of superiority, exclusiveness and safety similar to that provided by many sects that would be horrified by the comparison. What they have in common is a way to repair, with apparent strength, the fabric of social and spiritual life whose vulnerability it is unbearable to admit.

Tightly knit ideologies that evoke their own myths about reality and are coherent within their own terms (Nazism, Marxism–Leninism, absolute monarchy, absolute patriarchal religion and some forms of narrowly defined feminism) require a great deal of intensive education, control of debate and information, and the sanction in some cases of extreme violence because, ultimately, they do not allow for any reference beyond themselves. To allow that reference is implicitly to allow doubt about the system to bring into question the reality of the "myth spaces" that provide comfort and identity. Perception is controlled, but eventually the human mind requires a reference that relates to actual experience of how things are. The gap between allowed perception (and corresponding language) and the experience of the nature of people and climate and earth and love eventually becomes too wide to be denied.

For instance, crusaders who went to conquer the infidel and "liberate" the holy sepulchre were exposed thereby to contact with another culture, another faith. They met men whose courage, honor, and compassion rivaled or exceeded that of many Christians. Inevitably, many came home no longer able to accept the concept of one single path to salvation and the damnation of unbelievers. In this and other ways—the observation of natural things, and of the heavens, for instance—cracks in the walls of medieval European orthodoxy were made whose effects were gradual but enormous.

When the desegregation of schools in the United States forced black and white children to sit next to one another in school it did not destroy the racist systems—they were too solid—but it became impossible for at least many of these white children to accept the myths they had learned about what black people were like. They were too obviously just other children. The system endured, but weakened, operating effectively but undercover.

There are parts of the structure of human life that are essential; we cannot avoid them or make them totally adaptable to our preconceptions. We can reinterpret them to make them fit our myths to some extent, but there they are: death, for instance, or hunger, birth, sex, the climate, gravity. All of these—even death—we can to some extent modify to fit the needs of whatever kind of house we decide to build, but if we do so with enough disrespect for the reality we are modifying we end up having to create such a mass of extra props and distractions and false fronts that the sheer expense of upkeep becomes impossible to maintain, and the props and pretenses themselves begin to pull the fabric apart.

Disrespect is the word I chose to use because it does not imply that we have to (or can) understand fully the nature of the materials and elements of our building. You don't have to understand the molecular composition of stone to build a stone wall, but you do have to have a working knowledge of how the stuff behaves, and if you treat it in an arbitrary way the wall will fall down. (When I was about five, having learned that boats, although heavy, can float because they are hollow, I tried to make one by hollowing out a piece of soft chalk. It didn't work.) Respect for the materials of life means awareness of how things work based on experience, often the experience of many people. Disrespect means thinking that we can use the elements (materials? bits?) of our lives in any way that suits whatever myth-directed purposes we have conceived. Unfortunately, though the limits of this are fairly obvious in terms of literal building materials (if we reduce the strength of the purlins of a roof until they are too slight to carry the tiles, the roof will fall in) they are less obvious with the materials of life, and the results take longer to show, but the principle is the same.

When, in the United States, immigrant communities were deliberately discouraged by social workers (in the name of encouraging individual self-reliance) from preserving the close ties of extended family, and when, in England, people from bombed or "slum" neighborhoods were moved to high-rise buildings with no common space, in both cases it took a while for the weakening of the structures of community to result in an increase in the incidence of depression, crime and drug use—but not all that long a while. Disrespect for the nature of some kinds of reality means that our buildings won't stand. But when they begin to fall we can see where things went wrong, and perhaps do better.

Doing better, first of all, requires, as I suggested, that we understand the reason for the damage and the nature of the materials that have shown the damage. Doing better, however, requires more than information and remorse; it requires imagination. It requires that we be capable of envisaging not just repair and restoration but change, and this chapter, as well as spelling out the nature of some of the damage, has looked at some movements that envisaged and embraced change. On the one hand we have the awareness of a badly damaged structure, on the other the demand for very different spaces of living, and all around us is the awareness and the effects of cultural change so rapid and undermining that it seems impossible to imagine any kind of continuity. So the demand splits between the desire to preserve, patch, rebuild anew, or perhaps just camp out indefinitely. Yet there are those "bits" of our lives that are a given, and must be taken into account in any imagined structures, however flimsy.

Is it possible to be aware of the inherited structures that are part of our cultural psyche (whichever culture we have inherited) and yet to reimagine the spaces we inhabit in ways that fit the new thoughts and conditions of our lives? We live in a world where language has been shaped by a taken-for-granted separation between the material and the spiritual, between physical and mental, and we struggle to express in that language the disintegrating conclusions of quantum physics, and "field" theory, in which there are no "things" at all, but only relationship, information, movement. We have to find a way to live in such a world. Perhaps the first thing we have to do is to find a way to imagine that still keeps us aware of the basic reality of our situation. But how do we know what is real?

In literature, the intriguing and illuminating quality of the writing of James Joyce depends on the fact that the writer cannot actually convey all the layers of symbolism, conscious perception, ordinary speech and practical decision that operate in any human mind, because the mind cannot cease its operations in order to observe itself. But by shifting and changing, digging and skimming, surfacing one kind of awareness and then another, a feeling is created of the strangeness and richness of actual experience, and the reader becomes aware of resonances and depths, revealing in a new way the tough fabric of human life—ludicrous, sacred, ordinary. Chronos breaks down into anachronism that in turn illuminates the chronos. In another medium the paintings of René Magritte that drop the spectator into unsuspected pits of visual awareness, or the play on perception between surfaces and image content in, for instance, the work of Jasper Johns, forces the use of a double vision; the visual paradoxes of M. C. Escher, too, are examples of the fact that coming up against the "edges" of what our minds can do may be the one way we make discoveries that allow us glimpses beyond those edges.

However, it is one thing to experience the gap in expected continuity that allows for vision, it is another to recognize the nature of the vision and perceive the possibility of making it a reality. To do that we have to have a language to describe the vision. The crucial, and extremely difficult, issue is that we actually need criteria to evaluate the language with which we are to express the vision; otherwise, as has so often happened, the vision can be shaped by any persuasive ideology. What I am beginning to explore in the following chapters is the concept of hospitality as a way of supplying a spiritual motivation, a moral category, and—most importantly—a language whose concepts are sufficiently concrete to provide verification of their truthfulness by actual observation of how they work out in practice. This business of using language that can express myth and symbol and yet be accountable in terms of daily life, memory and vision is brutally complex, but the complexity underlies every project of hope and courage, and we must not (in the long run cannot) build our home unless we understand the strangeness of our primary materials.

3

Magic Casements

*I*n this crumbling house, which threatens to crumble even the meanings we attach to the words that describe the experience, we may be able to discover a sense of the reality of where we stand by creating windows that allow us to imagine alternatives, even very strange ones—strange enough to encompass an experience of hospitality as the criterion for the building of human spaces.

If we are to move and change at all, we have to validate our experience, and the words we use to express it. A totally solipsistic universe is one in which imagination is paralyzed.

To begin the process of reimagining our house by making windows seems a very odd thing to do, when we aren't sure if the walls will stand up or if the floor is solid. But in fact it makes good sense. By the decision to make windows, we affirm that the structures we have inherited are not merely fantasy. We *choose* to assume that they can stand up while we cut these holes, and this is the kind of choosing that quantum physics has taught us to recognize as one that doesn't just observe reality but actually brings it into being: a possibility is realized by the choice to observe, and other possibilities are thereby eliminated. To choose is, in a sense, to create.

We also intend that the windows we cut shall be appropriate to the kind of building we already have. This is a "peculiar" idea, because the whole problem, as it presents itself, is that the old building has lost credibility. Why cut windows when the walls are doubtfully real? The point is that only by choosing to cut windows may we indirectly return credibility to what still survives of the old house. We do not do this in the old way, taking for granted the unquestioned solidity of the building, but

45

we do it by allowing ourselves to discover a new basis for understanding the reality of the habitation we have inherited.

To understand why we should or could make such windows
we need to pick up again on the basic but confusing issue of
the usefulness of language, to remind ourselves of the relation
between reality and language. Language determines how we
perceive our inherited habitation and live in it. In that sense,
language is our habitation. Each age, each culture, even each
family, constructs its house of language symbols that provides
security. These constructions make life possible, because
through shared symbols certain things are accepted as solid
and enduring, we can stand on them, be sheltered from the
elements, go about our business with confidence that these
walls and roof will be there for us, a place to come back to, a
home in which to find assurance and purpose. In this house
words mean definite agreed things that we need not question,
so that we may use our energy to deal with the questionable
things we may encounter outside. We *have* to have enough of
these safe and solid symbolic homes if we are to live and work
with a degree of hope and sanity. We have to be able to count
on concepts that support the fabric of the house.

The problem we face, as I indicated earlier, is that the
accepted forms of most of our language houses have become
weakened by all kinds of attacks. The sexual revolution
(including contraceptives), the contradictions between the
massive commercial success of capitalism and the extreme
moral weakness that it can't quite conceal, the moral vacuum
created through three generations by the experience of too
much horror and too much institutional deception about it
(wars, genocide, nuclear diplomacy, support for economic reasons of dictatorships based on torture and corruption), and
the resultant collapse of credibility in major religious and political bodies, with the threat of lethal environmental changes as
a constant background: all this has deprived our western society (and most others) of the possibility of massive consensus
on what things are certain, right, wrong, important, eternal.

Beyond this and underlying all this and still not consciously
appreciated is a fundamental cosmological shift that has come

about in less than a hundred years. We still talk in terms that imply a universe conceived in Newtonian terms, a dualistic universe in which there are distinct bodies pushed around by certain "forces," such as gravity, none of it affected by a spiritual reality that emanates (if it does at all) from a separated God who manages the machine from afar. Talking a language based on this kind of cosmology makes no sense in a universe discovered to consist not of separate objects, but of fields, of particles that are also waves and can become one or another by an observer's choice, a universe of chaos that turns out to have an inherent order that we cannot predict or control, so we end up talking non-sense—but we have no choice. Our language hasn't caught up yet and is only just beginning to try to do so.

To an extent this has been mitigated in practice by our inheritance. In some places the old language houses still appear to stand. Many middle class families, and working people in traditional neighborhoods, still live (with modifications) in language houses built by their parents and grandparents and great-grandparents. Some expectations, some self-consciousness, have been handed down. The walls are fairly solid, even if there are cracks; the door, though it lets in drafts, still closes against the wind; the roof may leak a little but it keeps out the rain most of the time.

But things that have happened to people, cities, nations, have made much more serious holes in the old fabric. If, for instance, massive unemployment comes to a city because industry has moved to some place where people are willing to work for starvation wages in unsafe conditions, some of the old fabric of the house is likely, if not to collapse, at least to show severe cracks. This happens because in such an instance the experience demonstrates to those who lose jobs (and with them a whole way of life) that the motive of business that had supplied this livelihood and self-respect is basically greed for profit, and that politicians follow business. Inherited beliefs in justice and democracy are eroded, as well as the traditional conviction that people only become poor when they are lazy. What symbol system can be used to replace such a loss? A profound restructuring of language is needed—about patriotism, about community, about class. The Marxist analysis—the old refuge of critics of the status quo—offered a language to talk about all this, but it has lost credibility also, for reasons connected not so much with its internal consistency as with the nature of historical events and especially with the realization that people can be as corrupt and greedy in a socialist state as in a capitalist one.

When faith in the inherited myths is eroded so quickly and brutally, the materials for a new and realistic restructuring of a symbol system are lacking, and the gap is often filled with blaming of others (people on welfare, foreigners who take all the jobs) or with some kind of escapist religion, or with simple cynicism or apathy.

A similar erosion happens in the case of many single parent families. Women bringing up children alone may try to do it by attempting to live in the "house" they have inherited from a culture whose language symbols about family, at least in the last two or three generations, are based on two parents who are expected to be self-sufficient emotionally and financially, though they may include grandparents and cousins if convenient. This structure is itself a product of the economic requirement for the mobility of skilled men. It was created by political and social pressure and accompanying rhetoric and myths, and it required the isolated self-sufficiency of the family unit that follows the man to where the work is. There is no way a single woman with children can build a symbol-home in such a structure. To demonstrate that they can manage, many women drive themselves to combine school, work, and parenting, and try hard not to give in to the feeling that a single mother will never be quite good enough because she is only one. She suffers from stress, and may take on a man to give herself the illusion of being a "real family." Some women, with good family support and with enough awareness of the reasons for the choices they have made, emerge not only with greater strength but with a new critique of inherited social norms, but for many, without the self-confidence or the tools of analysis, it can seem that whatever they do, they will never be quite free of guilt, never be fully accepted, and their children, instructed by the culture around them, will learn to blame their mothers for whatever goes wrong with their own lives. In such cases the inherited symbol-structure about family does not protect a woman or make her feel safe or encouraged, and she shivers in the leaking, crumbling structure that she tries constantly and vainly to repair.

The inherited language about family doesn't work anymore for most families, whether they be single parents, heterosexual or homosexual couples, or "complex" families of divorced and remarried parents. None of them can live in the old house, yet their efforts to construct new ways of thinking and speaking about family are still judged by their resemblance to the old model. It is hard to move beyond it, but many do so, and so are part of the effort at a shifting vision and newness.

This failure of the effectiveness of inherited language systems as solid, secure homes enabling individuals and groups to function and interact harmoniously is, of course, not a new phenomenon. As cultures rise and fall, as refugees flee or immigrants arrive, as groups once oppressed become dominant, as agriculture flourishes or fails, as industry attracts labor or abandons it, people's view of themselves is changed, often catastrophically. The language by which they build walls around themselves, to define and defend themselves, to decide where the doors are to be and who can come in, is radically changed.

There is always an overlap as they adapt. When the machines took over the craft of the handloom weavers and the workers were driven into the cities to seek work, they took with them country attitudes, remedies, family structure, the sense of community. It took a while for these things to be lost in the struggle to stay alive. When people from Italy, Poland, Germany, filled the boats that carried them to a new land to escape oppression or in search of prosperity, they brought with them their own traditions, values, inherited skills, social expectations—their houses of language. These lasted a long time, and helped to sustain immigrants through hardship and hope deferred, but they changed too. There were new expectations, new values that many deliberately adopted in order to prove themselves Americans. Each house changed its shape and, at least, its paint, the second generation strongly repudiating the symbols that had still been needed for security by the immigrant parents. This new generation discarded skills, speech and customs, only to have them reclaimed by a third or fourth generation because such things, after all, could provide an identity and a place of belonging when the WASP culture made it clear that no amount of assimilation was enough to let any other ethnic group live in that particular mansion. But if this overlap experience of language "homes" changing has been a constant through history, there are two reasons why the situation now is so different that it seems to have shifted into a new paradigm.

One reason is, as I suggested earlier, the speed of change that is connected to speed of communication, so that people are more quickly and more widely affected by the events that may influence their ways of symbolizing themselves in language. The other reason, linked to this, is that the experience of radical and deeply disturbing change happening very quickly and repeatedly has made many people feel that, in a sense, there can be no secure language houses at all. If I perceive that other people's descriptions of themselves (the self-respecting industrial worker who counts on a good wage for his skill, the family that looks like the Waltons, the business man with a heart of gold, the faithful wife, the honorable soldier, the loving father) can be totally destroyed by loss of a job, by the drug culture, by the exposure of corruption, or by sexual abuse, then the floor I stand on suddenly seems shaky, the walls that protect me develop cracks, and I wonder if any structure is safe—or *real.*

What is so frightening is the creeping sense that almost any description of what we take to be reality could turn out to be illusory. If what seemed so solid is possibly just a hologram, a fleeting conjuration (however scientific) rather than a solid house, then life is indeed desperate.

Words have no meaning of their own; they are given meaning by the way we use them, and the meaning can change, as any dictionary will attest, but when the change is slow (who cares if "agony" comes from a word Homer used to describe a meeting for discussion, and "nice" once meant "fastidious"?) words are reliable enough for all practical purposes; they refer to no reality but the needs and viewpoint of the speaker or writer, the family, the national or religious propaganda, even though we continue to rely on familiar language for all ordinary purposes. But "reality" can seem to be itself a verbal construct and therefore subject to the same insubstantiality that mocks attempts to pin down experience and share it.

One philosophical view, referred to earlier, was developed to express this experience, under the heading of "deconstruction," and is a valid response to a cultural experience, but is also itself a symptom and result of that experience. It expresses the sense of lacking foundations or walls for our lives. It is a description of what it feels like to be linguistically in a state of flux, with no valid criteria for evaluating even the flux—its speed, direction or content.

The experience is connected to the underlying phenomenon to which I referred earlier—the cosmological shift that restructures any possible description of reality that our inherited language is able to handle, and leaves us fumbling with concepts that don't seem to fit our experience. That "experience" itself was and is in its turn structured by the inherited cosmology and the languages that grew to express it, so no wonder we feel like giving up the struggle.

But human beings are so made that they require concepts with which to orient themselves—they need the house of language. Can this only be a matter of temporarily agreed fantasies? Must we attempt to achieve social consensus on desirable illusions and hope that enough people will believe in them at a time to keep the business of living from dissolving into madness and despair?

The use of the image of architectural adaptation and change gives hope that there can be a way of living with the awareness of linguistic relativity that is truthful, and in truth grounded in a reality we can relate to. Although words are in constant flux they fluctuate around events that happen and are seen, heard, felt, smelled, tasted. We need words to make sense to ourselves of such sensory experiences. A very new baby's eyes are able to "see" anything an adult can see, but it lacks the information that would give meaning to the visual input, so in another sense the baby does not really "see" it. Equally, words without sensory reference, direct or indirect, convey no meaning. Yet, we deeply want our words to be what philologists call "isomorphic with reality," as things that, through long association and use, are not merely usable as convenient symbols but have a very close one-to-one relationship with whatever they are used to refer to. We need to believe that there is some kind of inner consistency between language and the facts of our experience. It is the attack on this consistency between language and reality that makes us feel as if our house is falling apart. Whereas, in times and places of slower change, the experiences and maturity of a person or a group—even a culture—could allow word and thing to develop a relationship, and allow it to shift with time, now the shifts are too fast, the changes too big. A gap develops in the house of language that cannot be passed over. But it is possible that, as I have suggested, the cracks in the building, which we are forced to acknowledge and try to rationalize, can themselves show us a better way.

Through those cracks whose existence we accept with such pain and grief we may still be able to perceive a different and possible experience of reality. We can go further—we need not wait for cracks to occur because of eroding experiences. We may do what this chapter proposes—cut windows, on purpose, to allow us to *look deliberately and freely at new possibilities.*

There could be a number of ways of exploring the alternative reality that we perceive through the new windows, a number of ways to reinterpret the house they illuminate. My own way into it is by way of the words of a poet. This choice is made because poetic speech is possibly the easiest way, the alternative being reliance on purely philosophical argument. Poetry confronts the inevitable prolixity of philosophical exploration (dealing clearly with unfamiliar conceptual dynamics requires a lot of explanation and a special vocabulary) and somehow collapses it into tangential allusions which, though not replacing the labor of philosophy, work just the same. Poetry dances through philosophical discussion without disrespect but displaying, apparently without effort, the psychic awareness that is in question. This happens because poetry actually demonstrates at an extreme point that inevitable transmutation of word meanings that happens in the normal processes of communication. It attracts or even drags out forcibly the associations that make words resonate with unexpected emotions. ("Yoked by violence together" was Doctor Johnson's disapproving comment on this process as exemplified by the metaphysical poets.) Poetry situates the hearer or reader at the point where different realities are exchanged and reveal new possibilities. But it also helps to strengthen—or even to repair—the sense that words can indeed be "isomorphic with reality." It gives the words, in their context, a power that is near magical in shaping how we experience the phenomena around and in us. It gives the courage to hope—not for any specific outcome but in the possibility of truth.

Rudyard Kipling wrote a short story inspired by an experience of the very early days of radio. In it the author sits with a wireless amateur, in a little room behind the pharmacy ("chemist" in England) where the radio enthusiast works, and hears him picking up Morse messages between fog-bound ships in the English Channel. But the chemist's assistant, working in the shop itself, is a consumptive young man who writes bad poetry and takes opium pills to relieve his tubercular cough, and is also in love with a gorgeous girl. In a semi-doped state, drugged with passion and opium, and in the course of a long, foggy evening interrupted by few customers, the young man sits by the stove with his notebook and begins to scribble unexpected phrases. Looking over his shoulder the author realizes that he is writing down scraps from the poetry of Keats. Does the young chemist's assistant know what he is doing? In lucid intervals it becomes clear he doesn't, though he has heard of Keats, who was also a chemist's assistant, and also consumptive and in love with Fanny Braun. Do "like causes produce like effects"? Does one consumptive, lovelorn chemist's assistant pick up messages from another, as the wireless receiver picks up messages from distant, unaware, ships at sea? As the excited wireless technician urgently tries to engage his literary friend's attention to share the excitement of being in touch with other minds across the miles, Kipling describes how he irritates the enthusiast by remaining in the shop because other and stranger communications are reaching across generations rather than miles. Finally, hesitantly, a phrase at a time, the dying man who is the receiver writes out two lines from Keats's "Ode to a Nightingale."

They are so famous that they have, perhaps, lost some of their resonance since Kipling quoted them—but never entirely, and only as long as we experience them as a "quotation." The quote on its own—the two lines—began in the middle of a sentence, so that we might not even know what it was that

> Charm'd magic casements, opening on the foam
> of perilous seas, in faery lands forlorn.

The agent of the "charm" is the nightingales's song:

> Perhaps the self-same song that found a path
> Through the sad heart of Ruth, when sick for home,
> She stood in tears amid the alien corn;
> The same that oft times hath
> Charm'd magic casements....

Kipling's way of embedding the lines in his story is not irrelevant. The story is about the threshold on one side of which we think we know where we are and can control it, while on the other side we can only guess, symbolize, wonder. Magic casements are thresholds between worlds but not doors through which we can pass. Kipling's sick chemist touched the threshold but did not know it. The wireless amateur thought the threshold could become a causeway, and in his own terms he was right—it has become the "information highway" of modern technology. But Kipling, who touched poetry himself in some of his verse, knew the proper nature of thresholds. More pertinently, so did Keats, and those lines provide a way to recognize the purpose of not merely looking through the cracks in the old walls but cutting windows, thoughtfully and with awareness of the vistas and possibilities. However, these are particular and peculiar windows.

"Magic casements" are windows created by processes that are unusual, perhaps seldom recognized as effective in some definitions of reality. But, however unusual, they are created by human design and control. Any window is created for human purposes, and the making of magic casements is an important and fully human function. In Keats's poem the agent of this magic is the nightingale's song that breaks through what had seemed to be a dead and near hopeless reality and allows the mind and heart to conceive of a different possibility. It motivates the magic of imagination that creates new visions. The sense of engulfing meaninglessness that characterizes our culture and drives people to such desperate denials and evasions can be breached by some experience of hope that liberates the magical power of imagination. Such an experience as, in this instance, the nightingale's song has to have a recognizable emotional significance and relevance. An act of kindness, a phrase of music, an unspoiled landscape, a meaningful experience of worship, a snatch of poetry, can do it, as well as more obviously powerful events such as sudden illness (or recovery), loss (or gain) of livelihood, the experience of war, birth, death, personal or communal danger or relief from it. Suddenly the old ways of thinking cease to seem inevitable; it becomes possible to imagine something new.

Some young architects in Boston, who, like so many, can seldom find enough commissions for interesting projects to build, created a group called "Artytects," whose purpose was to influence architecture by devising projects that would probably never be built but could fire the imagination of both architects and public. In an article about them in the Boston Sunday Globe, one was quoted as saying that "When you do imaginary drawings you're making propositions about what the world could be like." What can be imagined can become reality. Those drawings are "magic casements."

In imagining something new we are cutting windows, but we are standing within the old house as we look out through the windows. These are "magic casements opening on the foam of perilous seas, in faery lands forlorn," and what we see is not a space we can move into. These are windows, not doors, for one thing. They are indeed, like all thresholds, places of danger and of opportunity, literally liminal experiences in the sense explored in Mary Douglas's classic work *Purity and Danger,* and since recognized by studies in myth, psychology and spirituality. These thresholds of the spirit mark a point of initiation, when choices have to be made about how to deal with what is seen: to reject it as unreal, to treat the thresholds as an invitation to regions of magic power, or to recognize them for what they are—not doorways that human beings can pass but windows, and very particular windows, thresholds of the spirit only.

What we see through them are "perilous seas," and these seas are themselves part of the landscape of "faery lands forlorn." The sense is very different from the way we talk about a place being "like a faery land," implying delight and pleasure and beauty, insubstantial perhaps in terms of "the real world," but not dangerous. Keats views this realm as "perilous" and "forlorn." Faery lands are perilous and forlorn for human beings, as True Thomas in the ballad discovered when the "Queen of Fair Elfland" invited him to go with her. Like others remembered in song and legend one can dwell in "faerie" land a day and return a hundred years later, one may eat a delicate banquet and lose human form. The folk who belong there are, of course, quite safe; it is only dangerous to humans. So, if we may only move into it at our peril, what is the use of seeing it through the magic casement?

For Keats, knowing the approach of death, the power of imagination was to achieve a brief respite from reality, and it compassed the possibility of "easeful death," "to cease upon the midnight with no pain," as compared with the torturing progress of disease in an unhomely world. But the visions of a warmer, vividly delightful place which the nightingale's song made possible was an affirmation that life did not have to be as he found it— "the weariness, the fever and the fret, Here where men sit and hear each other groan ...When but to think is to be full of sorrow." Keats assumed, as most people do, that the fantasy was no more than that: once over, nothing had changed, it was merely a respite. Yet it changed him, as much as he allowed it to.

The importance of the view of faery land is that it gives the freedom to imagine what has not been possible within the confines of the old structure. To climb out and try to inhabit the faery land is indeed perilous, it means alienation from the human and a loss of the possibility of effecting change. To attempt to swim in those seas is to descend into psychic depths from which rescue is very difficult (though it can happen). But to lean out of the window is to taste the freedom of fantasy, to explore the images of faery land, to learn to perceive our own situation in a new way, and therefore, if we will (and it is a decision we have to make), to conceive of different ways of building the human house.

But perhaps the most important function of magic casements is that by choosing to cut them, and look out of them, we can validate the practical reality of the floor inside them on which we stand, and of the wall in which we cut the window. The very act of making and opening the magic casement and leaning out toward that strange view is an affirmation of the reality of the experience that confines us, but which can be changed. It is the experience of the distinction, the felt difference, between the fantasy and the experience of here and now, the existence of the threshold between the old battered house and the land of faery, that enable us to know that the floor we stand on is *not* in "faery lands forlorn" but, by contrast, is within the human realm, however damaged, and therefore within human ability to understand and to change.

Poetry, among other things, opens the magic casements we need because, as I suggested earlier, it uses words in ways that create a link between experience and feeling by way of association, making them "isomorphic with reality." This works because the words refer to memories of real events and experiences and so can create a fantasy—that is, an imaginary construct with real inner consistency—powerful enough to allow us to build up a whole alternative world. What happens when we open magic casements is that words are allowed to pick up resonances freely, new ones and old ones, and create alternative worlds of possibility.

A couple of different ways to appreciate this connection

come to mind. One way to help us recognize how fantasy—what we perceive through the magic casements—works to move us to desire change and believe in it is to understand how it works in the making of stories that engage us in an unfamiliar, even fantastic, world. In a later chapter I shall be using two of these—one "true" fantasy, the other actually historical. If they are well made they engage us deeply, and we are stirred to fear, grief, laughter, hope, joy, about events that either never happened and couldn't happen, or are strange and distant enough, historically or geographically. We believe in that world, and care about it, and in order to draw us to this, the story-teller must lead us to believe that there is a total context for the story itself, and that context must ring true to us in its own way as much as our own does. Tolkien, writing *The Lord of the Rings,* provided maps, genealogies, glossaries and supplementary stories about a history "preceding" his tale. He created the impression of a story with a solid context, and he did this throughout the whole book by matter-of-fact references to events that are in a sense unimportant to the "plot," such as references to old or peripheral customs, to stories and events familiar to the characters in the tale but not to the reader. In a different way Beatrix Potter did this in her stories about rabbits, mice and pigs. They wear unlikely aprons and waistcoats, and sleep in beds, but their quasi-human behavior is perceived in a way consistent with the predicaments of real animal lives: Peter Rabbit is in danger from Mr. McGregor, the gardener; Hunca Munca the mouse warns her babies against the trap set by the children's nurse; Squirrel Nutkin narrowly escapes being eaten by Old Mr. Brown, the owl. Beatrix Potter makes the fantasy work by assuming our own associations with comparable human predicaments, or creates a taken-for-granted context that is not described but only referred to, as when we notice that in Mrs. Rabbit's kitchen is a picture of a pie, which commemorates the fate of Mr. Rabbit, deceased, whom Mr. McGregor *did* catch.

Another way to understand how fantasy emerges from the known and especially from the past is the way in which some women, seeking ways to revalidate the female experience, and so to find words to help rebuild the crumbling human house, have looked to ancient women's occupations as ways to understand their own gifts and powers. The idea of *weaving* has proved very powerful in evoking the power to make a single and strong fabric out of many threads, and even to make with them pictures and designs that record, remind, inspire and teach. Linked to this is the idea of *mending,* in the sense of weaving threads into a hole in worn fabric, to make it whole again. Few women in western culture nowadays have woven anything more ambitious than a pot-holder made on a toy loom, and most don't even know how to darn a sock or a sweater (they are taught to throw it away instead), but the image of the handloom weaver is still powerful. And a significant, though still small, number of women in western nations have chosen to revive the craft and even to make a career of it, as many still do in countries in South America, Africa and Asia, and indeed among Native Americans who preserve or revive their own ancient methods of weaving.

Even women who do not themselves know how to weave understand the process, one that actually happens. So when, for instance, a book of feminist essays on ecological and environmental issues is titled *Reweaving the World,* women know what that means. The word has great power because it has a real and verifiable reference. More than that, the reference is to a craft that requires great skill, which has scope for much artistry but can also be done at a very simple level. Besides, it is one that is not the secret of a scientific or social elite. Though levels of achievement will vary, the qualifications for the craft, once it is reclaimed from the factories and their mindless operations, is simply the will and the skill to learn it, perhaps even to the point of building a loom. This "weaving word" evokes a whole alternative world, a context that is part history, part fantasy. It doesn't have to be described in detail, or analyzed, or researched; it is simply a vision through the magic casements, but it is coherent; it has the power to create not only nostalgia but energy and hope. It suggests the ability to cross lines of class and education, it evokes thoughts of hard work, patience, experience, and a product that is beautiful and enduring (and capable of being mended!).

There is more still to the view of "weaving" through the magic casement. This particular word needed to be rescued from being either a technical word about a process of manufacture remote from the designers or the users, or a tourist attraction, or a bit of exquisite nostalgia or artsy-craftsy irrelevance. The rescue was possible because of those women who found the magical power to open the casements and to experience weaving and mending as things that go on in faery lands. (Perhaps the ships on those perilous seas carry the precious webs woven by faery women.) This made it possible for them to discover a whole new and empowering significance in the words *weaving* and *mending.* They are grounded in inherited fact but capable of nurturing the same kind of skills, patience, energy and artistry in the service of essential tasks to be used for mending and reweaving a whole culture.

This happened because the view through the magic casements was intellectually coherent and therefore emotionally powerful. When the women in peace camps wove colored wool into the fences around the sites of nuclear weapons, everyone knew what that meant, and it was very threatening to the servants of destruction. The word and the fact had a deep relationship and it moved as poetry moves.

Magic casements are not permanent windows. They do not look out upon earthly views; through them we cannot look at the passers-by or the neighbors' homes or distant farms or mountains. We also need "real" windows, but the "realness" of "real" windows, like that of the whole fabric of our house of language, depends on the ability provided by magic casements to envisage things we don't otherwise see at all. Casements open outward; they are not sealed storm windows nor sashes that go up and down. Casements allow us to lean out to feel the winds off the perilous seas and glimpse far-off shores of lands that we shall never inhabit. Such windows have always provided a means of survival for the human spirit. From Keats via Anne of Green Gables, to Tolkien and Ursula LeGuin and *Star Trek: The Next Generation,* the fantasy world is not merely an escape but a place to discover values and meanings that make possible the building of a truly human habitation.

The whole notion of magic casements suggests once more that, in the task of making choices about the future of our habitations, the most important tool is imagination, but imagination used in a certain way. It presents us with possibilities that inspire us because they are based in verifiable experience. Like the architect's experience and skill that "can make propositions about what the world might be like," these possibilities also allow us to change and be transformed, to take on forms we had never thought of, to shift our paradigms and experience the familiar as strange, the impossible as normal. (As a scientist pointed out, someone who was asked to hoist several tons of water into the air without visible support would conclude it was impossible. But every time we look at a cloud mass we are seeing just that.)

As we explore ways of reimagining our structures, our homes, languages, habitations, philosophies, families, religions in order to create a hospitable house for all earth's creatures, we shall need to keep in mind the uses of magic casements and the importance of that coherent imaginative context that we call fantasy, so that even the most apparently "fantastic possibilities" may engage us in real action.

4

Upstairs, Downstairs

*T*his chapter is about what our culture has learned through millennia to think of as our "lower nature." These are the things we have culturally either suppressed or oppressed or hidden, for various reasons, and yet this "underneath" area has been a constant, no matter how described, condemned, used, abused or explored.

An example that has rocked the self-satisfaction of western society is the newly publicized horror of sexual abuse by people our society has been taught to revere—clergy, therapists, teachers and others. The more the subject has been researched, the more it has become clear that this is not new, but in the past the victims were more often forced into silence by fear or, if they spoke, disbelieved, or blamed, and even punished as witches or as psychopaths. Freud's now well-documented cover-up of what he knew of child sexual abuse helped for a long time to label the disclosures as the sick fantasies of children or women. Being forced to deal with the evidence as reliable, and to do so in public, has been traumatic for the whole society, and already the backlash is trying to push the disclosure back onto the victims, calling them liars or fantasists. To acknowledge what is "underneath" can crack open the depths of a culture, and it then becomes clear that our house is built on damaged foundations; we need to understand that in order to learn how to build better.

Not all that is "underneath" is evil—indeed what is uncovered as evil may sometimes only have become evil because it was hidden and we know so little of the reasons for human evil. "Underneath" us are the places of inspiration, prophecy, the places of beginning. One thing is clear, and that is that the regions under the public floors of our house are places that can put us in touch with realities that can be ignored only at our peril. When we examine them, reluctantly or eagerly, they reveal to us parts of our human building that are simply irreducible, no matter how denied or feared.

If the building is to stand up and provide a human house, however adapted, and for whatever changed purposes we intend it, we need to know that bits of building, which kinds of structural engineering we absolutely have to have. Since the underneath is also the foundation it seems an important place to explore.

"Underneath" in some sense is, besides, the place where we encounter and deal with the most awesome, the most basic and also the messiest aspects of human life—the experiences of sex, birth and death that open up depths below polite exchanges. "Underneath" too, in more modern structures, is where we deal with human waste when it becomes unsatisfactory to dump it in the fields or streets. What any society (or class or family) chooses to keep "underneath" is probably the best indicator of its values and priorities. For all these reasons an adventure into the "underneath" regions—a mental and spiritual adventure but also often a literal exploration—is essential if we are to understand what is involved in changed criteria for human structures in all aspects of life.

It only becomes possible to undertake such exploration because of the awareness discussed in a previous chapter of language as a building material. But in exploring the "underneath" we are moving into an area where we have to deal with something beyond language, or at least beyond "Words, words, words"—the realm of symbols, myths, pre-literate experience. To open our magic casements is to expose ourselves to the power of ancient divinities, and it is only with their help that we can first imagine and then build the house of every day. They live, in civilized cultures, mainly in the regions under our floors. Children, still, sometimes take care not to tread on the lines between street-paving stones; you never know what lives under there and may emerge through the cracks and catch you unawares. If the view through magic casements empowers imagination to visions of real possibility, then the search in the deep places can put us in touch with some conditions for realizing our visions, namely the regions of human and earthy life from which power is released, as we may recognize it in faery land, but so as to allow it to operate within the very real human house.

When a house has been neglected the obvious damage will probably be to roofs and windows; water gets in, walls have damp patches, vandals have smashed windows. But the canny surveyor, estimating whether repairs are possible and how much they would cost, will look at the floors, to see whether there is extensive rot and what state the foundations are in. The uninformed visitor, less experienced, may step on rotted boards and discover, rapidly and unpleasantly, that what goes on under the floors is important.

This doesn't necessarily allow us to suppose, however, that when the foundations of a society have been damaged the obvious answer is to re-lay the floor of our own culture as before. To re-lay the foundations as we imagine them to have been is the solution proposed by some Christian traditions, with varying degrees of subtlety, and by governments. These, observing rotten floors, feel a need to deflect blame or responsibility from their area of possible action and propose as scapegoats some segment of the population (Asians, young black men, people on welfare, drug addicts, single mothers, gay people, etc.) as those who caused the rot. This tends to preserve the foundations of western capitalism from too much inspection. Although replacing the floors will not do anything but cover up once more the rot that has penetrated below, and will in time re-emerge, the last thing the preservers of law and order want to do is examine what is underneath.

The rebuilding of the foundations of a large structure is obviously difficult, but it has been done in recent years. Among the most notable examples was the complete excavation and replacement of the foundations of the vast medieval structure of York Minster in England. It involved putting the whole building on temporary supports while the foundations were carefully dug out, examined, and replaced by new ones. In this process, the remains of older foundations, including parts of the two-thousand-year-old Roman regimental headquarters, were excavated and preserved along with artifacts from many intervening periods. Information about the earlier history of the building was accumulated, and in the new foundation a museum was created to allow visitors to "walk through" the centuries of change in the Minster and the city it served, a remarkable instance of the deliberate creation of opportunities for "shifting vision" of past and present juxtaposed without absorbing one into the other. Since then, other churches and ancient buildings have similarly been given new foundations, often in such a way as to allow earlier history not only to be recorded but afterward to be "visited" at will.

This is the kind of undertaking that seems to be indicated if we are to make the future foundations of our structures durable; indeed the example I gave at the beginning of this chapter is not the only one that has made western society pay attention to what goes on under the floor of everyday behavior and consciousness and has made it clear that the foundations of the cultural psyche require massive repairs to the point of replacement. One of the conclusions drawn from the digging and delving that has already been done is that we need to be aware of what goes on under the floor, whether we think of it as the place where the plumbing goes, or the region where the servants live, or as a place to put stuff we don't want and a probable haunt of mice and black beetles, or of something more universal, necessary and dangerous. There may be no ghosts in the cellar, but perhaps we shall meet our ancestors. The plumbing that keeps our houses clear of our waste products is not mysterious or disgusting but the work of knowledge and skill, and if it goes wrong the results are unpleasant.

Opening up the foundations of a building also allows us to be aware of the actual processes of building, and thence to imagine the reasons that led to the building, the attitudes, beliefs, concerns, that influenced the designers. Can we imagine living in the kind of building these builders regarded as normal and necessary? If not, what has changed? Why do we now need to lay different foundations?

We need to undertake the journey downstairs, and indeed this exploration has been going on for some time. The speculation and interpretation of psychoanalysis and especially the

Jungian versions of psychic journeying all indicate the special importance of the journey into the depths, though mostly as an individual project. Using the image of a building suggests that it was the rottenness of the floors, making them unable any longer to support daily life, which actually prompted all this psychic archaeology.

Once, on a journey through the mountains of West Virginia, a friend and I came upon a place where the whole of one side of the road had fallen away into the valley below. A notice in front of the gap read laconically, "Single line traffic only." Similar tactics had for long enabled the traffic of society to negotiate the presence of rotten patches and holes in the floor by going around them, refusing to recognize in them the result of a disintegrating structure. At about the same time (the late nineteenth and early twentieth century) as the delving into the subconscious was beginning, however, the same holes in the floor were prompting inspection by social reformers—socialist, feminist, Fabian, anarchist or plain Utopian. The "holes" indicated by such things as infanticide of illegitimate babies, back-street abortions, industrial and venereal diseases, strikes, prostitution, and cholera epidemics in western cities motivated concerned people to explore the underside of a superficially extremely prosperous and "progressive" society, but they did not compare notes with those who perceived the same "holes" in different terms, those who delved down into the individual psyche that could be and was also expressed as referring to whole ethnic groups or nations. These psychic diggers had also been aware of the previous avoidance of holes, but saw this avoidance in terms of the denial of sexuality, the fear of feeling and of the body, the attempt to deal with strong passions by suppression or by displacement onto people of other races or classes. So the exploring of the foundations in society and in the psyche went on more or less at the same time, and the tearing away of rotten floors was undertaken with glee and much self-righteousness but by separate and often rival teams of excavators.

The social reformers and the psychologists not only did not compare notes, but each group also regarded the work of the other group with distrust and contempt as a facile response, the one party maintaining that no genuine social transformation could take place without psychic transformation, the other regarding the pursuit of personal wholeness as a middle-class luxury that distracted from the search for a new world order. At this point, at the end of the twentieth century, it is clear that both of them were wrong. Personal transformation does not happen in isolation, but works itself out in relationships and in the context of hopeful work and sane lifestyle. And social movements founder unless they allow for the psychic and spiritual needs of people who cannot be satisfied to be purely servants of the future.

We have torn up the floors to examine the extent of the damage, and we know we need new foundations and, like the repairers of York Minster, we know we must build them without destroying the whole building—which means ourselves and the whole culture. We are also aware, by now, that simply to repair and then close up the spaces underneath will not do—indeed we probably can't do it. Yet it doesn't seem satisfactory simply to remove all the excavated rubble and remains, leaving only massive concrete and steel supports in view. The foundations of human life are not like that; there are always more things we don't know, but with which we can be in touch through the signs of the past. To go down under the floor is to go back to the places of beginning.

The places of beginning are linked with obvious practical purposes because they are also places concerned with the most basic human and earthly functions: with the growing and preparing of food, with all the mud, blood and sweat involved; with digestion and evacuation and ways of dealing with the results; with menstruation, sex, childbirth, and in all these with the endless cleaning processes—exhausting, messy, repetitive. One woman, remembering her experiences of the then prevalent model of modern childbirth, commented bitterly that "they were only interested in me below the waist," for our kind of culture is anxious to separate "higher" from "lower" functions, and it has done this to the laboring woman—and often still does—by choosing to treat her body as a machine for producing babies. By dealing with her "below the waist" in a mechanistic (though "kind") way, those in attendance can avoid dealing with the dangerous symbols of this experience of origins. On the other hand the newly delivered mother, visited by friends, sits up in bed with the covers drawn over her belly. It is now allowable to be interested in her feelings.

I shall be returning to the issue of birthing as part of a reimaging of the "lower" regions of our habitation, because it is one of the most powerful of symbols, having to do with mystery we can never entirely "medicalize," that which underlies all of life, not only "beginning" in the chronological sense but origins, below the levels of consciousness. Just now, and as one way to begin thinking about what is "downstairs," I want to remember the power that has been attached to birthing as a symbolic as well as a physical beginning.

Birthing is as old as the beginning of mammals, and it happens every day. Its power and awe were once worshiped, and later they were feared by the worshipers of new male gods who got rid of that numinous fear by denying the worth of women. The power of the symbol of birth would not go away, but it could be controlled. Athena, great goddess of Greek patriarchy, was not born of a woman but sprang fully armed from the head of Zeus, proving that for the higher things a woman's womb was not needed. In the Christian tradition, even as the transforming images of birth and death were brought together in the baptismal rite, the fact of women's birth-giving power was subtracted from it. To women was allowed by the Christian churches a birthing without power or mystery, a birthing into sin and death, from which the child she bore could only be rescued by a spiritual birth conducted by males. Yet even this was too powerful. In the baptismal rites of most traditional churches of today there is no journey downward into the regions of danger, but only a quick dipping or pouring of water. The colder climate of northern Europe may have had something to do with a reluctance to plunge the neophyte bodily into deep water, but the effect was the same! Whatever the theology said, the symbols had forgotten the dark journey through death to new life. There was only a kind of washing; the emphasis was not on rebirth but on cleansing from sin.

Remembering this, we recognize that we shall need to make the significance of baptism available to everyday living in the imaging of the human home. Going down into the water under the floor means not only "being open" about those aspects of ourselves and our society that were and often still are kept out of sight, literally or socially, whether it be menstruation or sewage or prostitution or AIDS or death. It has to mean also an ability to acknowledge that we are entering an area of mystery, where easy notions of good and evil become confused. We can touch the source of those fears that have not only allowed but required the marginalization and exploitation of women, the distortion of men's affect, the flight from compassion.

The symbolism of the regenerative water is that we dare to descend into the dark, under the surface, to places where we are not able to see clearly or know where the bottom is or even if there is one. We can perceive shapes and movements in the water, but the essence of the experience is that we are willing to touch and be touched by things at the roots of being, not just as individuals but more importantly as a community of live creatures.

True symbolism helps us to transcend the categorizing of "higher" and "lower" regions as respectively spiritual and earthy, not to say dirty. But the reason why we need to recover the sacredness of the "lower" is that the suppression of what belongs to the "lower" as inferior if not actually evil is embedded in the culture of the west and in its language. We have inherited the assumption that "civilized" societies (that is, societies centered on the "civis," the "city" on the Greek patriarchal model) separate higher from lower functions, and the naming of some as "low" indicates that they are to be transcended as far as possible by people who want to live noble and spiritual lives. This is done by keeping the lower functions separate—verbally and spatially. Some are not referred to, some are relegated to special places, Caste and some are assigned to special classes of people who are thereby classed as "lower" and therefore appropriately concerned with "lower functions": peasants, servants, women. It is interesting that in our modern reaction against some of this we refer to the importance of "getting your hands dirty," meaning a

willingness to engage in tasks usually assigned to inferiors—that
is, the people who *normally* do "dirty" work. Even the American
use of the word "dirt" to refer both to what is unclean (including
morally unclean), and to the stuff from which life comes, indicates this fear of our origins. For we think it "dirties" or "soils" us
to be in contact with these beginnings, the underneath places.

But our society's struggle to transcend its "lower" nature
means that it not only assigns certain functions to "inferior"—
which, of course, means "lower"—people but also needs to *keep*
them "lower." As long as we can only respect ourselves as
humans when we are about "higher" things, the "lower" ones
are a threat to our humanity. The people who attend to lower
things become themselves not only inferior but somehow less
human, and not only less human but dangerous. There is always
the pervasive fear that they might break out of their proper
sphere and attack our superiority. Slaves may rebel, workers may
strike, women may invade the places of power, black families
may move into our neighborhood. Careful structures of expectation and control are therefore put in place, to persuade the dangerous ones that *their* "place" for "our" purposes is where they
should be. And when they do surge upward in a way perceived
to be threatening, the reaction is violent. We need only think of
the sadistic violence toward the Suffragettes in Britain, which
was actually official government policy—the tearing of their
clothes, the handling of their breasts by police, the forced feeding—and also the panic measures used against early unionists
and present day migrant workers in the United States.

The much loved TV series *Upstairs, Downstairs,* was a marvelous illustration of how this worked at one particular time.
Those "downstairs" people were literally under the floor upon
which "real life"—the noble and significant life—was going on.
Without the labor of the "downstairs" people the "upstairs"
life could not go on, but that labor was hidden. When the servants came "up" to clean it had to be at times when their "betters" were asleep or out of the room that had to be cleaned.
Servants might serve the food prepared "downstairs" but not
speak to those they served at table unless asked a question.
Their attic rooms were tiny, barely furnished, unheated, their

wages miniscule. If accused or dismissed, they had no recourse.

This was all part of the system that allowed everyone concerned to accept this separation as in the nature of things. It was widely accepted by the "upstairs" people that servants did not have "finer feelings." The eighteenth century view of the "lower orders" was that such people were virtually a different breed, incapable of a high level of moral, spiritual or intellectual achievement, though their submissive labor might earn them an eternal reward. This class attitude was so strong that an upper class person could actually feel disgust at being touched by an inferior, which was also why servants in genteel households wore gloves to serve at table. In some very expensive restaurants they still do. The same feeling among white people (which in some places still exists), that the touch of a black person is contaminating, is one example of a social phenomenon that is only indirectly a matter of color. Class, which is essentially the separation of "higher" from "lower," is the operative dynamic.

It was, of course, only possible to create a series like "Upstairs, Downstairs" and other similar dramas when times have changed and few such households remain, at least in the west—it still goes on in sections of some Arab societies, for instance. But our ability to be fascinated by such a class structure, and to congratulate ourselves on our more egalitarian outlook, can enable us to avoid recognizing the significance of that particular stratification.

Our idea is that now *everyone* can live upstairs. We have brought it all into the light. We can talk about sex and birth and death at dinner parties, cultivate our own gardens and do our own cooking with pride, and put all the dishes in the dishwasher. We can even clean our own toilets. But we also do our births and deaths in hospitals, have our food processed in factories, our animals killed in abattoirs. (A young woman accustomed to eggs in boxes from the supermarket was offered some new-laid eggs by a neighbor who kept hens. There were a few feathers stuck to the eggs. Her reaction, once the donor was out of the room, was one of disgust: "I couldn't eat *those*—I want *real* eggs!") We work hard to make sex, birth and death as unmysterious and impersonal as agri-business tries to make food production. Our grandfathers and grandmothers lived upstairs or downstairs, while we deny the existence of downstairs until we fall through the rotten floor.

Downstairs is still there. If we have opened up the floor and called the downstairs people to come up, we are very unwise if we simply seal off the disused back stairs, substituting one kind of denial for another. The regions under the floor are still dangerous to us if we insist that there is no danger and that we can deal with all that used to be underneath by hauling it into the light. We can't do that. The origins of our being are below the floor, and can never be completely brought upstairs.

We need, therefore, to look at the holes in the floor, and look through them, as the repairers of York Minster did, and find ways to enter into those dark places, not accidentally when the floor gives way but with deliberation and yet with a certain fear, because we are going down into the places of beginnings, and we shall never fully understand them.

We need to find a way to descend into the regions under the floor with understanding and with awe. When we return upward we need to carry with us the experience of recovering our beginnings.

I return to the obvious image—obvious to the point of seeming trite—the image of baptism. Baptism is not a Christian invention; its symbols emerge from many religious contexts, but Christianity has made it a central and essential symbol and therefore has studied and practiced and reflected on the symbol and the rite more than most. In the symbolism of the baptismal descent, birth and death are experienced below the level of every day, below the floor, but the place of baptism is visible; it is secret and yet public. This is possible because the foundations have been laid open, to be visited and revisited, and since they are open they are visible, and the way in which they are part of the building is visible too. When we rebuild our foundations, perhaps we need to build into them such a place of public baptism so that we can go downstairs with deliberation as a way to newness, not to forgetfulness. The shifting vision we make possible by such an excavation is of the coincidence of mystery and practicality, an awareness of how the plumbing works, which is also an act of reverence for the vast subterranean interconnec-tions that make renewed cleanliness possible.

Baptismal images are about birth and death and derive their power from that encounter of extremes, so baptism can only unfold its meaning when we recover the sense that this sign of spiritual regeneration depends on women for its meaning and its power. We are back at the beginning, and the beginning is a woman giving birth. In the murals of Catal Huyuk in Anatolia, painted six thousand years ago, the awesome power of the life-giving and death-bringing goddess was depicted as she was in the act of giving birth. In the design of some old homes in New Eng-land a room was routinely included that was known as the birthing room. It was in the middle of the house, and it was kept as the special place where women gave birth. It provided some-where apart, a place of women, even though the birth took place literally in the center of the household. Birth was—and still is in more "primitive" societies—an event with strong psychic power, and care was needed both to protect the mother and child from evil influences and to protect others who might be vulnerable to the gathering of power around the birthing. Margaret Meade, in her studies of Samoan tribal life, recorded that, in some groups she studied, children fell into a deep sleep when a woman was in labor, a kind of defense mechanism against influences with which they were too psychically immature to deal.

Only a few generations ago, when home-births were the norm, men were not present at birth (except for upper class women who had doctors) but neighboring women—women of the family and the local midwife—surrounded the woman in labor who was the focus of attention as she worked to bring forth new life. She needed this support because she was in a place of danger as well as joy. She was afraid and she suffered; she needed help to support her courage and endurance and to celebrate her triumph when the child was finally born. Birth is close to death, and the fear of death in childbirth was, and still is, very real. We now prefer to deny this, and so we often deny the woman the release of being able to acknowledge fear and receive comfort, but now as in the beginning the experience of birth challenges the power of death.

The experience of every woman who gives birth is the earthing fact that allows us to understand some of the meaning of the baptismal journey. When we reimagine and refound our house of habitation perhaps we should not close over those foundations but leave them accessible. Perhaps here, already, we have an indication of what the concept of hospitality might do to our attitude to the lower regions. Does this access to what is below have to be a wide opening, perhaps a pool with steps down into it? Or a narrow stairway leading down to the place of wisdom? As we go down, will we discover paintings on the walls, left by those who passed that way long ago? (This is an old house.)

As "chaos theory" has explored, chaos is not, in fact, a random, pointless confusion but a process, a movement of inherent though unpredictable order. Chaotic systems, however, did not fit the given scientific and cultural categories of order, so for long we could not use them to understand our reality. It was our fears that made chaos fearful, because its power, which we cannot predict, it a threat to our control. The ancient myth of Gaia symbolizes the struggle between the "family" of Gaia and the male gods. In the myth that has been filtered through the later patriarchal systems, Gaia, the earth, the mother of all, gave birth to Uranus, the sky, and she became also his mate, with whom she conceived the seas and mountains and all the earth, and many other strange offspring. The whole tangled myth of origins then shows those other children of Gaia—monsters such as the Titans and Cyclops, who are presented as deformed, gigantic and dangerous—warring against Gaia's son and mate, the sky-god Uranus, but especially against Zeus, who had subjected their mother to his rule. In the end the earth-mother, with all that she signified, was altogether displaced by the new, male pantheon in which the goddesses were merely subservient (but occasionally spiteful) hangers-on. But Gaia did not die or change into a submissive consort. She simply went underground. She was to be encountered in the places of cthonic (earthy) power, the caves and shrines of the oracles, even if the power was claimed by a male god, like Apollo at Delphi, who still needed the female pythoness to utter the oracle. Sometimes these shrines were openings whence flowed springs of water, as if the goddess were still giving birth to the new life. People came to her in secret, seeking wisdom in her deep heart, seeking healing of body and mind, seeking comfort and hope.

When the culture of Greece had been passed on to later patriarchal cultures, when the sky god was not called Zeus but perhaps Jupiter, the caverns of the earth still sheltered the mother goddess, as they had done in Israel's history when the sky God was Yahweh. Later, in western religious myth, she appeared to children and peasants, and healing streams once more flowed out of the depths from her womb. She was called Mary, and was hailed as mother of mercy, virgin most renowned, seat of wisdom, health of the sick, comforter of the afflicted. Still from beneath the ground, as at Lourdes, came hope for ordinary people who found little comfort in the rigid legalities of patriarchal religion. But for this very reason those manifestations of mercy were suspect. So when huge popular support and the outpourings of healings and hope forced the official church to recognize the presence of divine power, it was quickly co-opted. The crowds were organized, the healings categorized, the water itself fed through taps and into baths so that it could not flow in unauthorized channels where anyone could wash or drink unsupervised by authority. But the water flowed, the people came, the power and mercy would not die. Deep underground, the power of the origin of things was at work.

In her book *The Mother's Songs,* a wonderful exploration of personal and cosmic symbols in picture and memory, Meinrad Craighead, artist and mystic, tells of a dream she had when she went on pilgrimage to Einsiedeln in Switzerland, where lies the tomb of her name-saint, Meinrad, and the shrine of the black Madonna. This is how Meinrad tells the story:

> Above the candles, above the eyes turned to her, stands the small Black Madonna of Einsiedeln. Swathed in a jewelled satin cloak, her face a dark hole in the surrounding brightness, she is enthroned on the crescent moon.

> I stay the night in a local Gasthaus and I dream of the Black Madonna. I have wandered into a remote hill village, a random assembly of poor, white-washed stone huts. Women are scrubbing linen, kneeling at a small rocky stream which twists over

stones, glistening in the sunlight. I pass slowly through narrow, dusty lanes, moving without direction, stared at by children. I am content to be in this place. The path ends abruptly at the entrance to a cave. An attempt has been made to provide the hill's gaping hole with a portico entrance. There are a few pots of fresh flowers. This cave is being cared for. I step inside the entrance, adjusting to the sudden darkness.

Groping through a twisting tunnel I perceive an object ahead, a dark triangular bulk filling the innermost chamber. She sits immobile on a roughly hewn stone throne. Her body is darker than the close dim interior, darker than the stone throne. Between her arms on the arms of the stone throne, her lap spreads out, a receptive center, a protective oval. I stare into the bulk which appears to be both convex and concave. I gaze into her bigness, her oldness, into the broad lap where all the darkness is focussed.

Suddenly a young girl appears at the side of the throne, crawls familiarly into the lap of the Black Madonna and vanishes into her embrace. Within the same movement I am drawn forward, understanding that I am this child. Discovering the Mother, I find myself already with her.

Here is the fullest experience of the pilgrimage into the origins, the womb of life, the universal places of darkness, whose power centuries of patriarchal religion has tried to make fearful, places to be avoided as evil so that, in the event, they become evil. The images are powerful to help us understand how we need to be in touch with depths that are not of themselves evil but certainly awesome. The way to the shrine, for instance, is through everyday life, but this is of a simple, pre-industrial kind, where strangers are normal and welcome and, in the sunlight, daily life goes on, including the wonderful work of everyday cleansing in the waters that themselves emerge from the darkness. The shrine is a cave in primeval rock, yet the entrance is marked and it is cared for by humans, and it is open to those who come, it is not private or defended. The Madonna herself is dark, undefined and yet central, and the one who goes down into her also enters into the depth of the self. The personal journey downward is an ancient path to the places where life begins, and ends. This is the place of holiness. As in the symbol of baptismal experience, it is the waters from the depths that regenerate, but the way there is not by secret, elite initiation, but by simply choosing to go, as others have gone.

All this holiness emerging from under the floors is without words. It comes from the origins, the places and times when there was no language in the sense of recorded words, for words only happen when they can be written down. Before that there is speech, but it is re-created at each use by memory—Mnemosyne, that daughter of Gaia whose myth has nothing to do with history. Mnemosyne reminds, hints, images, calls. She precedes the muses, who inspire the arts of civilization. They are her daughters, but Zeus, the conquering sky god, is their father. With them, human knowledge and skill are inspired and organized under patriarchal rule and are capable of being recorded, not merely remembered. That is how knowledge comes to us, including the knowledge of what we call myths. We read about them, and reading and writing are things done "upstairs." When we go "downstairs" we enter again the place before language, the place of myth and story and image that Plato described as suitable for the illiterate—children, poets and old women.

This presents us with a real problem. We cannot return to a pre-literate past; we are people who read, however uncritically and unprofitably. The myths themselves do not come to us as shared and fleeting stories, renewed each time uniquely by the story-teller, or in drama and rituals designed to evoke the memory that cannot be captured. Instead we study them as objects of learning, trying to discover the ancient wisdom that we feel we need. But it is no use pretending that we can shed the accumulated effects of millennia of culture, of literacy. Even though the literate have lived "above" a continuing popular subculture of "superstition" and "magic" and legend and have drawn on it even as richly as Shakespeare did, it is literacy that shaped and shapes the way people are allowed to think. The suppression (the word is accurate) of non-literate cultures has been virtually total in our time. The remaining ones are endangered and indeed often themselves aspire to literacy for the sake of survival. That older and "lower" cultural mode has gone for good.

(If our culture is destroyed to the point where all records disappear, our descendants—if any—will not be able to draw on the ancient continuity of mythic sharing. They will, unimaginably, have to begin all over again.)

Our legacy of literate culture is built into our pattern of thought as well as speech, and this has made possible the huge achievements of civilized historical time. We can't undo that even if we wished to, yet we know that our culture, suppressing all that is strange and dark and beyond patriarchal control, has endangered the whole structure of earthly life, "high" or "low." The symptoms of the danger posed by the attempt to deny or obliterate the "underneath" or "earthy" things have been and are such things as the drug trade, the Nazi horror, the frantic pursuit of wealth and possessions, and the abuse of children and women and any who are weak and in their vulnerability are trigger to the "panic" fears of loss of conscious human control. "Panic" is the effect of contact with Pan himself, the great pre-literate power of the untamed places, and he drives to madness when he is denied and suppressed. In Europe he survives as the "Green Man," a male face made of leaves or pouring vegetation from mouth, nose, even eyes, turning up carved on misericords and corbels in churches, even on western secular public buildings, as a kind of subversive reminder of an older religious sense even in Christian times.

Some images of the Green Man show him grieving, as for a great loss, but we can't become pre-literate, we can't live "downstairs," abandon "upstairs" life as too dangerous and become "in-sane." We may rightly grieve, but we cannot go back. So we need a way to come and go, to enter into the place of origin, not as anthropologists, studying the ways of alien cultures, or as psychologists and psychoanalysts, seeking to understand individual strangeness and make use of it, but as pilgrims. As pilgrims we seek access to the holy places in order to continue our lives, healed and encouraged, and knowing we cannot fully understand or map the places we visit.

The places we visit are there because the divine power of the beginning was at work long before we built our structure of civilization on top of it. But they are also there because we made them. We made them, sometimes, as places of imprisonment and forgetfulness for "lower" people and functions, but we made them—without fully understanding this—also to become the symbols of individual sacramental death and birth. And now we have to open up ways to them, deliberately, as a means to save the structure, not so much of personal life as of the entire culture—if there is time.

The enlightenment philosophy of the late eighteenth century attempted to eliminate darkness and mystery and only succeeded in making it evil, but the post-enlightenment European and American cultures have not been the only ones that denied darkness. The Greeks and Romans (among others) did so too, and the classical revival was part of the enlightenment agenda, for good reason. Those classical cultures had developed systems in which slaves, servants and women dealt with the "ignoble" aspects of life but in which, also, cults of mystery, most often located or celebrated in caverns, grottoes and underground chambers, offered escape from the unbearable light of patriarchal righteousness. These were not all women's cults, although many were; the Roman military followers of Mithras sacrificed the bull whose blood poured over initiates in the cave beneath and, earlier, men and women came to consult the pythoness at Delphi in her grotto. And all the places of underground worship were places of pilgrimage—places to go to and to return to the light above, but also places to come home to in the sense that the devotee was returning to the origins, the places of primeval wisdom, of birth and also of death, the passage to the underworld, the inescapable commonality of all life that begins and ends in the womb of the earth, and between the beginning and the end must seek wisdom if it is to grow in the daylight.

Western culture has gradually and reluctantly been driven to question and reject aspects of its enlightenment legacy, but not before the foundations had begun to fail as the building above grew more grandiose while no one paid attention to what held it up. So when we come to reimagine the foundation, we cannot just imitate the old; we need a new kind of space, and yet it must serve the old purposes as well as the new ones. So we may return to the image of regeneration, of rebirth, a different kind of baptism, and the creation of a place for it, perhaps quite literally, in the reimagined house of humanity. We recognize that, unlike the traditional theology of Christian baptism, this isn't something that happens once and for all. It has to be repeated many times, though there must be some point of decision. The point of decision is, in a sense, the moment when it becomes acceptable and usual to "build in" to the floor of everyday conscious living this way down to the places of origin. But we can't, as the early church did, build a separate baptistry in which to enact a once-for-all sacramental rebirth. Our baptism has to be ongoing.

In Catholic churches there are, or used to be, little bowls of blessed water near the door into which the faithful can dip their fingers on entering and bless themselves as a reminder or re-enactment of baptism. This is a way to make "ordinary" and ongoing the baptismal experience. The emphasis of this particular symbolic act is more on cleansing in order to enter the holy place than on the image of death and rebirth, but still this is a kind of mini-baptism, and the bowl is a mini-font. Yet in another sense it is misleading, a kind of avoidance of the real challenge. These "fonts," like the bigger ones in most churches, are above ground; they belie their name. The "font," the "fountain" of regenerative water, springs up from the depths; we can't command it, we can't tame it, or make it a piece of domestic equipment, or even an ecclesiastical one.

Part of understanding how this works is recognizing that the water was always there. We didn't dig a hole and fill it with water like a swimming pool; rather it bubbled up from deep down, and filled the space allowed for it. We often think of "fountains" as artificial structures fed by piped water and used to decorate parks and gardens, but the fountain is originally a spring, pushing its way up to the air from the heart of the mountain. It is a curious fact—coincidental or serendipitous as we choose to think of it—that the tributary stream of the River Thames called the Fleet and which once flowed through London was covered over, and later the Fleet Prison was built above it. Nowadays only "Fleet Street," once the home of so many newspapers, still reminds Londoners of the underground stream and, if they are knowledgeable, of old ways of dealing with "undesirable elements." It is true that mostly we didn't in fact give the "fountain" space to emerge and flow visibly; we sealed it away and used our "lower regions" to accommodate what we didn't want to acknowledge—servants, refugees, prisoners, sewage. The living water seeped away or was turned into a sewer, as in the case of the Fleet, and emerged somewhere else, unnoticed.

But even when we dig the holes that allow the springs to emerge once more, we can't follow the springs to their sources. The sources are sacred, dark and far beyond our understanding. They were there from time immemorial, and are also part of human beings because we are part of creation. Touching back into the places from which these fountains come is something we need to be aware of, not just on special occasions but constantly. We need the shifting vision of Kroll's adaptations.

This was perhaps not so necessary in times and places in which people were (and some are still) in touch with the origins in various ways, as part of a mainly agricultural society.

Rituals and celebrations of the cycles of growth as well as the familiar yet mysterious experience of fertility made it more difficult to avoid the awe of the deep places. Modern western agriculture is designed to separate people from the symbolic implications of the processes of growing food and raising animals; everything possible is done to make farming as alienated and alienating as a factory production line, so we seldom look to rural life to feed the spiritual hunger of the cities. As production of actual food becomes less human, more processed, the food less nourishing and more likely to be toxic, so the spiritual significance and power associated with food-growing and eating declines. It becomes essential, therefore, to undertake a deliberate search for the places of origin, and a deliberate rebuilding of access to regions once familiar. Where the mysteries are not encountered in the normal order of things we have so to arrange our lives that we do encounter them, or risk falling into the disaster that we ourselves have created out of our fear of losing control.

The image is of the provision, in some of our cultural houses, of openings to allow descent to the places below, where the fountains have been given space to gush up and fill the hollows. With them, strange memories and powers emerge, never quite seen but dimly recognized by half-caught resemblances to dream figures, mythical beings, ancient tales. It won't do to build swimming pools with steps and bottoms you can see—if there is a bottom at all it fades away into the dark openings of unexplored caves. Perhaps we need steps, to let ourselves down slowly, but we also need the shifting vision: the awareness of the old floor that has been pierced, as well as the living water beneath. By some unevenness of the edge, by the broken end of a beam of wood or concrete, we need to be reminded that there was a break, that the floor that our ancestors built, and which we lived on, unheeding, for so long, is still there, surrounding the hole. Our ancestors made mistakes, we make mistakes; we thought we could live on top of the earth's deep, dirty original places and be forever above such things. We actually did it for a while, and the culture that lived like that was and is real, and had and has its achievements, one-sided and flawed though they may be.

ᵗ No more than we can safely replace the old floors and seal off the downstairs can we return to a religious culture that was in touch with the origins because it had never discovered any other way to live. We have discovered other ways, and for good or evil we have built on that discovery the vast edifice of a world in which technology and the people who manipulate it for their own reasons control the globe. But it is also a world in which the communication of music, visual arts and all kinds of thought and inventions has created a network of minds seizing new visions and rediscovering old ones. We cannot go back and weave our lives around the hearth, guide our ways through the rituals of the goddesses, live by the cycles of seasons and stories. We cannot unlearn it all even though we recover older ways of knowing. When we do learn the older ways it is not in the continuous web of tradition handed down from parent to child, elder to younger, but by a break with later tradition, a decision to find something else.

That is why we need the shifting vision. And the shifting vision has to be public as well as personal, built into educational and religious systems, a part of the worldview that may still, conceivably, save the human race and enable it to live a little longer on this planet. It can be done. A remarkable example is the rapid growth of "Revels," an organization dedicated to creating seasonal celebrations in song, ritual, story and dance, begun twenty-five years ago by John Langstaff, who has devoted his life to sharing traditional song and story. Presented in more and more U.S. locations by a mix of professionals and (mostly) amateurs, including children, "Revels" draws on traditional cultures and attracts thousands to enter into ancient rituals; myth; games for the winter solstice and Christmas, for spring, for harvest. "Revels" is a public yet deeply personal, sacramental experience of old and new, humor and drama. It draws modern audiences into participating in the shifting vision that allows them to be in touch with origins, and return with hope and a changed perception of reality. It is a pilgrimage, "downstairs" and upwards, linking people with ancestors, gods, and themselves.

The thing we learn from such a pilgrimage "downstairs" is that in our rebuilding of the human habitation we not only can but must keep referring to those human facts that are irreducible. Birth as we have seen is one such fact, one such experience. It is only one, but it is a place to start, since we must start somewhere if we are to move toward real transformation and a recovery of what is "downstairs." Beginning there may even enable us to understand better how to reshape our experiences of the other "foundation" things—food, earth, death, sex. It is a fact of origins, of beginnings, in every possible sense—socially, physically, spiritually, politically. It is dangerous because it is ultimately uncontrollable in its symbolism, yet it is also the ultimate source of hope. If it lives with death (and both live "downstairs"), it is the foundation. The alienation of the modern birthing process is not merely a tragedy for individual women, it undermines the whole building, connected as it is to the alienation of what is "downstairs." To honor the places of birthing as sacramental is to rebuild from foundations—foundations of respect for the past, for the mysteries, for both sides of the brain, even for the one-sided achievements of western culture that include methods of saving many mothers and babies from death, but that can be judged by new criteria and so used in ways that allow the shifting vision.

After strange explorations, memory comes back to the level of everyday living, the floor on which we live, and recognizes that if the traffic of earthly life—of humans and non-humans—is to continue, it must be built on foundations to which we have access when necessary, so that we can *see* where we come from. Birthing symbolism is not the only possible one, but it is a foundational one, and it provides a kind of moral reference point. As we treat birthing so we treat the earth and all of life. Whatever demeans, conceals, distorts or trivializes women, death, childhood, physicality, food, age, also does these things to the concept of process, and therefore to the possibility of hope. Birthing earths our judgment and therefore our decisions, in the foundations of our being.

Birth is also the point of possibility, the point at which no walls or doors have yet been designed, no inclusions or exclusions determined; options are open. This is why it is essential in some sense to experience rebirthing if we want to shape the structure of life according to the new—yet very old—criteria of hospitality and discover what that can mean, spiritually and practically. That thought brings us to the realization that— apart from the nature of the protection a dwelling provides— the most significant thing about any structure is the ways in and out of it, the entrances and exits. The next chapter grapples with this fascinating and elusive reality.

5

"...Every Exit Being an Entrance Somewhere Else."

*T*he point of this book is to suggest ways in which we can reimagine the possibilities of the structure of our houses in realistic and sustainable ways by understanding how the situations, the "houses," of our lives are built and therefore how they can and can't be altered without disaster. Fundamental to this exercise is the ability to switch imaginative concepts, as Lucien Kroll does in reimagining the function of an old building. This chapter explores the question of such imaginative switching, using the categories that emerge when we think about human action and the spaces for that action in terms of appropriately placed roles—that is, action as *acting.* It is about playing roles, about the "stage" on which the acting is done and about the relationship to this of "audience" and "backstage systems."

This takes the discussion not so much a step further as perceived from a different point of view, that of the actions within the spaces—upstairs or downstairs. It gives us another way to recognize possibilities, not only by cutting magic casements but by being aware of another kind of magic—that of the stage and its illusions that are so real they can change a culture. The "Revels" referred to in the preceding chapter are an example of this.

A stage is a place where people adopt roles in order to work out a story, a philosophy, even a theological description. By doing this the actors create an illusion, but they—and the audience—know it for illusion, yet demand of it reality. But what of all those not on stage? Where are they and do they matter? Who is "on stage" and where? Who are the audiences and what are they for? Can audiences and actors switch roles? The thresholds of a house (real or metaphorical) are both exits and entrances—but in which direction are they entrances onto the stage where the significant things happen? And when are they exits into the dimness of "backstage" which only exists for the sake of the stage? Which is illusion and which is real? For the purposes of this quest, the issue of reality and illusion is, as we've seen with "magic casements," reimagined, rebuilt. Illusion—fantasy—and in this case role playing are essential in order to perceive possibility. Only now we are thinking not about a whole faerie world but about real spaces in which illusion is created for the sake of truth, and about how people move in and out of those spaces, on stage and off stage.

In *Rosencrantz and Guilderstern Are Dead,* Tom Stoppard does his special thing of challenging assumptions so rooted in our speech that we don't even know they are there. In a theater the audience sees a certain space that is designed to create the illusion of (or at least to symbolize) a room, a garden, a bit of a battlefield—that is where the things happen that are presented to the spectators as "real." Whether the stage is a cart for the performance of a medieval mystery play, the corner of a street used by street players, or a sophisticated stage with all kinds of technical capability for "illusion making," the acting space is the place where significant action takes place—significant, that is, to the author and (so the author hopes) to the audience.

For the purposes of the play, that space is reality. The audience knows perfectly well that when the players disappear through a door or behind a curtain they stop "acting"—that is, they cease to be part of the "reality" that is the play. But if any in the audience are thinking about that, it is in a separate part of their minds while their central attention is involved in the stage "reality" which in fact they know to be illusion. This is the shifting vision effect once more: the stage/audience relationship depends on the fact that the audience *both* knows that the splendid palace is made of painted canvas and is moved by men in jeans, and *also* believes in the reality of the passions of the princes and princesses, the villains and heroes, on stage. Both are present for a successful dramatic experience. The child small enough to be thrilled by seeing "real" fairies, or terrified by "real" goblins, has a very strong emotional experience but it is not a *dramatic* one precisely because the child does *not* know that the back of the fairy palace is only canvas.

But if both kinds of awareness are necessary, one or other is always "out of focus." When the curtain comes down for the interval we may talk about "technique" and "design," but when it goes up again those reflections are once more out of focus.

The actor leaves the stage. She or he steps through a door into "back stage" reality, into a non-place. As far as the reality of the stage is concerned the actor has moved from illusion to reality—the reality of his or her own life. The back of the set may be canvas and two-by-fours but it is the reality of an everyday life whose business it is to create an illusion of reality on the other side.

Yet the action on the stage is real. To the extent that the skills of players and director and designers can engage imagination they create reality. It can be real enough to incur lawsuits, real enough to challenge and change cultural attitudes. Which is real—the stage scene or the back stage scene? Are they both real? If so they challenge us to look at what we conceive to be real.

In the terms of the building that provides the conceptual tools for this book, the issue of exits and entrances is obviously crucial. In Stoppard's play, Rosencrantz asks: "What exactly do you do?" and the Player replies: "We keep to our usual stuff, more or less, only inside out. We do on stage the things that are supposed to happen off. Which is a kind of integrity, if you look on every exit being an entrance somewhere else."

What is "on stage"—that is, the real action, the significant people—from one point of view is "off stage" from another. And yet the people who are "on stage" because what they do is important and noticed are—by being "on stage"—cut off from the "real" world of those who watch. They are actors.

In a Victorian home, like the ones transformed by Lucien

Kroll, the "upstairs" people were the possessors, the owners, the ones whose roles made a difference. Their lives were "on stage" to their servants, their dependents. What they did and decided was significant, they claimed a reality, but it only existed as long as the imagination of the "audience"—those on whom they depended for their ability to continue in those roles—was engaged in perpetuating their reality by believing in it.

The children in their nurseries, living up above the grown-ups' rooms and bedrooms but below the attic where the servants slept, were audience from one point of view, actors from another. They were trained to believe in the central importance and inevitability of the "on stage" actors. One day they would be "on stage" themselves, and meanwhile they were given "bit parts" to help them learn the trade. But also they knew a great deal about the backstage life. They listened to maids and nannies and learned. They felt, even if they did not fully understand, the way in which the wonderful people on stage lived by an elaborate pretense whose nature they glimpsed through gossip and observation. They fantasized about being on stage, but also about escaping the roles they were learning. Boys dreamed of being grooms (free to come and go, spit, swear, wear a striped waistcoat), girls imagined themselves making wonderful cakes, able after work to sit by the fire in slippers and tell fortunes in the tea leaves. Children always know about exits and entrances, and they can deal with the ambiguity of the thresholds with ease and professionalism. They know that exits are an entrance somewhere else.

In some modern middle-class homes there is an attempt to assume that everyone is on stage. Kitchens open into living-rooms, children share grown-up space. But when guests are expected the toys are cleared away and the table decorated with candles and flowers and grandmother's silver. Young children are (if they cooperate) put to bed and the hostess changes her clothes. She takes off her apron and puts on fashion. The stage is set; the exits into dishwashing and motherhood are tacitly ignored unless the baby is teething. It is a game that everyone understands, and the boundaries are usually more for fun than deceit (unless the boss is coming to dinner) but it is significant that the fun consists in creating an illusion of a way of life in which certain things are not done by "us." The adoption of a common set of exits and entrances is essential to this kind of game, with the understanding that what lies beyond the exits is not only "off stage" but, for now, "off limits." The easier version of this playacting is when people go out to dinner, where they can be "on stage" without trouble, wearing their best clothes, being waited on and, for a while, having the illusion of never needing to wash dishes.

But what about the back stage people on whom the illusion depends? What about the point of view of the servants, the waiters and waitresses, or the hostess when she's still in her apron? What about the view from the kitchen, the nursery? In terms of social structure this means all the people whose poorly paid and mostly boring work keep the system going, but again the image of people operating in an actual house helps to make clear what is going on.

As with a stage play, the performance depends on the fact that the people who are back stage are convinced that they must continue to keep the stage action going. Their motivation may be financial, but not always. True, in the past, "downstairs" people stayed there because in the nineteenth and early twentieth centuries the alternative was usually unemployment and, quite possibly, starvation. Their modern equivalents are often aware of the same stark choice. The woman or man who plays the dinner party game may not be driven by risk of losing a job but of losing a certain kind of social acceptance that feels essential, and that is a clue to the other part of the motivation. The back stage people have learned to believe in the importance of what they are doing. The servants (and whatever they symbolize in terms of dependence in any system) have internalized the conviction of the central significance of what goes on on stage. They may hate it or despise it or admire it, but they believe that it is strong and will continue. Some of them, like the children, play "bit parts" on stage, bringing in the coffee tray, answering the door. Some actually aspire to "real" roles one day. But they all accept the fact that, for now, the doors onto the stage are, for them, exits from unimportance and entrances into the place where the important things happen. Their behavior and their conversation "off stage" center on what is happening in the play. But not always: when there is a crisis, when personal tragedy strikes, or good fortune happens (a lottery win, a wedding), the focus can shift. For a while the backstage person becomes an actor accepted as significant, the stage has moved, the green baize door to "upstairs" is an exit, not an entrance. But there is no permanent change. The "real" actors see to that. They notice the event, sympathize, offer help, congratulate, celebrate. So they make the event part of *their* performance, for as long as is necessary. Then things may return to "normal."

When there are riots in Los Angeles or Brixton, when an earthquake strikes, or when a new factory is opened in an impoverished area or a spectacular rescue is performed, politicians and bishops and royalty (if available) visit and are photographed hugging or shaking hands with the victims and the heroes and heroines; they express suitable sentiments and promise whatever action seems likely to gain them publicity and approval. (Their sentiments may even be sincere.) For a while the people directly concerned are on stage. But the "real" actors have made sure the play will continue to be their play. In the traditional English pantomime it was—and is, where it survives—customary at some point to invite members of the audience on stage, to involve them in the action. It's a lot of fun and it helps to make the show popular, but everyone knows that when the show is over the temporary actors will fade back into the nameless mass while the real actors and actresses get ready for the next performance.

There is an ambiguity that becomes apparent when we think about exits and entrances, which is that the roles of audiences and of back stage people converge. The play exists because the audience believes in it and is involved by it in creating an imaginative reality of a very powerful kind—that is, if it's a good play. The back stage people are engaged in helping to create the illusion/reality. They know how it works, they see the canvas back of the solid-looking stage set, but also they believe that it matters that the performance should go on. They want the audience "out there" to be impressed. They are allies of the actors as well as being, in the dramatic event, their subordinates; but they are indispensable allies and in some cases professional equals—people who do lighting and costumes, for instance. So the audience and the back stage people and the actors themselves are part of a three-way conspiracy to preserve the illusion that is also a reality so important that its destruction is to be avoided at all costs.

In real life (if I can even use such a phrase at this point) the roles are more confused, as in the example of the re-creation of illusion at a dinner party. In modern western culture there is an attempt to pretend that audience, actors and backstage people are all one happy family. We claim to have abolished class distinctions; in a democracy a bag-lady can talk to a president, a woman can run a company, a laid-off factory worker can complain to the nation on TV. The stagehands take a bow after the performance, some of the audience are invited on stage, or actors are "planted" in the audience. It seems that old limits have been breached, and so they have been, and the decision to do this (though it may be used in cynical ways to gain support) is the product of real change in the way people think about exits and entrances.

But when the lights go out and the theater doors are locked, the same people are in control, because they have to be, if the play is to go on, for good or ill. When they choose they can stretch the categories, but it is their choice, though the reasons for the choice can emerge from deep conviction or merely from a desire to keep the control.

It is their choice because the audience believes in what they are doing and wants it to happen. In Barry's *Peter Pan,* the fairy Tinkerbell, who is represented only by a little shifting light, begins to fade and Peter is afraid she will die, so he asks the children in the audience, "Do you believe in fairies?" On their answer depends the life of the fairy. If they answer "We do!"—as they always do—she will live. On the audience's answer depends the life of the drama, but as long as the audience answers "We do!" the people who make the drama are in charge. This applies to all kinds of situations, for the very existence of a project, mission, form of government or business depends on the belief in it of the audience. For instance the particular small non-profit organization with which I work depends for its continued existence and its mission on the "audience's" belief in its reality; this means that its "cast," its script and its theme must make powerful and consistent sense to its audience who are the people who ask for its help, volunteer, talk about it, give it money. The play, of whatever kind, expresses something about the nature of life that people need and want to believe in, and therefore, to whatever extent the "players" believe appropriate, also to take part in. And the audience, even if nobody joins the cast on stage, *does* take part. Without it there can be no play, as the Player says in Ros and Guil when his players discover, to their horror, that no one is watching them; the absence of audience deprives them, in a sense, of existence. But this horrified reaction shows up the importance of the existence of plays and the spaces in which they happen. These are the places where myths are formed and tested.

So which of us is on stage and especially—since we are all on stage in some way and in some aspect of our lives—when? We mostly do all the things theater people do in different aspects of our lives, but *how* we do each one depends on how clearly we recognize the location of the exits and entrances, and where they lead to, and from.

In a home such as the Victorian one I explored earlier, and still in some wealthy homes as well as in hotels and restaurants, the door between the kitchen regions and the main "reception" rooms (whether "upstairs" or on the same level) is a threshold that defines class and role. The "real" action is on one side, the upper class side; the "back stage" is on the kitchen side. But if we think of a traditional farmhouse, the categories are reversed. In older farmhouses, there might be a "parlor," used for weddings, funerals and on Sundays, as a kind of concession to the claims of gentility (a curious version of the take-off-the-apron game), but the real action unquestionably took place in the kitchen. People (that is, women) certainly cooked there, but everyone else ate there—owners and farmhands, children, visitors. They learned, quarreled, shared love and information, made decisions about the whole household, held gatherings for celebrations, for political purposes, for prayer, for crisis management. This was the stage, and everywhere else—even the parlor—was offstage. The farmer might have had an office somewhere, but the center of things was not there. This has, in fact, gradually changed, and is changing, to marginalize the rural kitchen and move the stage to the manager's or owner's office with its computer and its network links to bureaucracy and power (still very largely male though women do take on these roles), but this change in itself shows how important it is to understand where the "stage" is and what is the significance of its thresholds in terms of where the things happen that are considered to be important.

I propose to explore the implications of this elaborate social game in several contexts, which are distinct but inevitably overlap. The choice is wide but certain contexts of human life seem to present themselves at once. The areas of human experience referred to under headings of gender, of class, of religion, of employment, and of urban and rural planning all depend for their operation on unquestioned agreement about what is on stage and what isn't—that is, about which spaces are those in which the truly significant action takes place. If we want to reimagine the significance of certain groups and their relationship to other groups, then this kind of exercise can loosen up the imagination, liberate anger and hope, and energize toward action of an appropriate kind. It will also raise issues of ownership, and eventually of the possibility of thinking about movement between spaces in terms of hospitality.

To look at gender in this way is almost too easy to be fun. It is so obvious that women are mostly not in the leading parts and that most of their work and lives are off stage. To go through a door into a room associated with women's work— the kitchen, the nursery, the garment factory, the old typing pool (and its newer equivalent space for computer-servants)— is to exit the area of significant action.

One program designed to help women make the choices that can get them off dependence on welfare has taken as one of its basic tasks the facilitation of an imaginative switch. It leads them to perceive entrances into women's spaces as the thresholds of areas of important action. When women have been brought up to regard themselves as without skills or important knowledge they assume that the spaces in which they operate are off stage, outside the places where significant things happen. They assume that their role is essentially both supportive and dependent, and hope for recognition and acceptance through providing services to those "on stage" and because their dependence comforts the power-need of those who control their lives.

The imaginative shift required is major. These women must learn to perceive the typically feminine spaces as places where things happen that are of basic human importance, and to recognize that these spaces are within their control. If a typical perception of poor women is of themselves as unskilled, they can learn to claim that they have skills that haven't been recognized. For instance they may have learned to care for a sick relative, they may be good listeners, they may have taught themselves how to do home maintenance jobs, even plumbing and electrical repairs, they may have successfully grown vegetables, they know how to make children's clothes, they know how to budget, how to cook, how to tell stories. They can learn to recognize their skills of nursing, counseling, appliance repairs, gardening, dressmaking, child and home care as real, as skills that can be increased and made marketable. Suddenly women's spaces are places where important things go on, and it seems possible and worthwhile to cross thresholds into other spaces, not to escape from "back stage" to "on stage" but from one area of significant action to another possible one. This is not merely a question of ability to earn a living but of a shift from whatever is considered to be (and women often consider themselves to be) back stage, below stairs, or whatever other spatial metaphor expresses subordination and lesser importance.

The recent use in the USA of the term "the outer class" expresses with grim accuracy the situation of a growing number of people who have been driven beyond all the structures within which the rest of the culture functions. The threshold between these spaces and the recognized spaces has been virtually sealed, as a drawbridge to a castle was once lowered behind all "our people," to keep out an approaching enemy.

Most poor people (and I include working poor) are in a "female" category in the sense of providing essential support for the "real" action which is the prerogative of middle and upper class people. The fact that, in fulfilling the "American dream," some people can and do emerge from poverty (even, exceptionally, from the "outer class") and attain wealth and influence, or at least homeownership and a desire to vote, doesn't alter this; the class relationship remains unchanged, only the membership of each class changes slightly. Real change can only happen when the actions of poor people are seen as significant, first of all by themselves.

This kind of change happened initially with the various abortive and forgotten rebellions and revolts of the poor in Europe and in eighteenth century America. Few of these penetrated the history books. Major revolutions and rebellions—in England, in France, in Russia and elsewhere—began with poor people who saw themselves as powerless and wanted power, but they depended on the leadership of an elite who had the ideas and gave the orders and bestowed the illusion of real change, though the old systems were soon replaced under other names. Smaller rebellions, truly developed by poor and ordinary people, never had a chance, though their scanty records show some genuine rethinking going on. The Diggers, for instance, in seventeenth century England, had a real vision of an egalitarian society without personal ownership, in which common labor was the bond. They never had a chance to work it out in practice since they were violently dispersed after a few short months.

The trade union movement was a genuine grass roots movement that grew big enough and powerful enough to create political change, though internal weaknesses plus the power of big corporations and the decline of industry have increasingly marginalized it. But a reimagining of how power works is happening again now in many western nations as disillusionment with government and economic frustration drives people to organize, to create local and alternative institutions for housing, employment, child-care, health, and other needs. They discover that they have the skills to do what they had always been told had to be done for them, at the decision of the people with power. They can discover they have so much power together that they can even make a hostile, class-based system work for them without being co-opted. They have political skills, business skills, planning skills and more. They do not *leave* the physical or emotional space assigned to them as dependent and subordinate but they change its significance, so that it becomes a place where important things happen. They are "on stage."

Neighborhood organizations, for instance, have raised funds to buy and renovate hundreds of units of housing; they have created their own banks to lend money for small businesses, and have funded their own local clinics and child-care facilities. The Community Land Trust model, holding land for the community in trust while selling the homes on long leases, in one form of this. Grass roots groups are creating their own schools and even colleges, setting up community farms (local householders holding shares and receiving produce) and business cooperatives and other decentralized ownership models. These entities exist across the United States, in Europe, Africa and Asia. People who do these things no longer try first to move onto the state of recognized "public life," and then address the needs of "those people." They create a new play on a new stage, but that stage is exactly the same area (often literally) where they have lived their lives as back stage people.

From that newly interpreted space they can cross thresholds and operate in the spaces of other groups that have power. The exit from their old space is a movement from what is now a fully public and visible arena into others that are also public. They may even, in some respects, perceive the old dominant systems as useful sources of what supports them—that these can become "back stage" to them—but this is not really a simple role switch, more a pragmatic way of dealing with potentially intimidating power systems.

When the spaces assigned to poor people are transformed in this way (both symbolically and in a literal, physical sense) unfortunately the gender spaces are not always changed too. Working class movements have been notoriously sexist, and neighborhood organizing can often be created or led by women in the early stages and yet eventually be taken over by men. Women are fighting against this quite consciously, and some-times winning, but the fact that the struggle is still so intense has to do with the employment dimension of the discussion.

Occupations that are regarded as normatively appropriate to women—the spaces that are regarded as "feminine" in nature—are dependent and supportive, and non-public. Women who move into positions of control and public visibility move out of those spaces and enter the stage of significant action, leaving their old spaces unchanged; in the same way the expectation is that poor people who are unusually talented and energetic will become "success stories" by moving out of poverty, leav-ing untouched the structures that create poverty. But, as we have seen, if the women's spaces are reimagined as significant, that changes the way the whole "house" works, but this is not just a gender issue: poor people of both sexes change the way they behave when the things they do are recognized and respected as publicly important, but in the case of class divi-sion as opposed to gender ones the reimagining tends to cover things "normally" done by men: politics, business, major pub-lic decision-making. It fits the separation between the domes-tic (female) and public (male). In liberation movements the world over, even where much of the organizing, risk-taking and genuine leadership has been done by women, the assump-tion has been that women's needs and ambitions are subsumed in male-defined goals. Attempts to put forward woman's needs as part of the liberation agenda have been condemned by men as "self-serving" and "divisive."

In the early days of the trade union movement women who wanted to put birth-control clinics on the working class agenda were denounced because the male dogma asserted that a man with adequate wages could support "any number of chil-dren" and to limit pregnancies was to betray the cause. In the same way, in the 1984 miners' strike in England women spoke in public, stood on picket lines, organized feeding programs, were beaten by police and reviled by the public, but when it was over the Miners' Union was very unhappy with the new female visibility: the women were told to go back where they belonged. Writer and singer Janet Russell soon afterward addressed the issue clearly in a song called "No Going Back."

> Since the miners' strike has ended, a new life has begun,
> We're different women after all we've seen and done;
> We've learned the world's divided, and we have made our choice,
> We may have lost a battle but we've found a voice.

> Chorus: There is no going back, you've struck the women now,
> No going back, there is no limit now,
> No going back, you've got to win it now,
> No going back!

> Life's hard if you're a worker, it's harder if you're black,
> It's hard when you are old or poor or get the sack!
> It's harder for a woman when she tries to say
> That she doesn't think the kitchen sink is where she'll stay!

> Some families deny it, some families understand
> That a woman's rights are equal to the rights of man!
> So if you call me "sister" when I join your picket line
> Better be there with me, brother, when I fight for mine!

The reimagining of the significance of women's spaces is therefore a lot more revolutionary than simply redefining class space, because it involves reimagining the relation between kinds of employment, in the literal sense of what people do, not just what paid jobs they may have. The division still reflected in the common description of women who "work" as opposed to women who "don't work" says it all: women who care for children and elderly relatives, grow food, mend (clothes, plumbing and appliances), manage the household budget, transport family members, cook, clean, entertain, volunteer at a local shelter, sing in the choir and organize fundraising events for the AIDS Hospice—these are women who "don't work!" Women who *do* "work" but also struggle to bring up children and keep a home together are still not in the public arena because their employment is seen as secondary to that of those without other concerns than their career. Though this is changing significantly, as I shall discuss, it is still a common experience of many married women who have jobs that even sympathetic husbands take it for granted that if there is a conflict of time management (the husband is called in unexpectedly to his work on the weekend his wife is scheduled to give a two-day seminar) his work will take precedence over hers. She is the one who must cancel, or juggle child-care, or rush home between sessions and worry.

When women recognize the astonishing range of skills they possess, go on to acquire more, and reflect on their occupations as centrally significant human employments, then the results are potentially very far-reaching, precisely because these skills are originally "domestic." The revaluation of home-based skills means that the separation between "work" and "family," between "domestic" and "public," between employment ("stage") and home ("back stage") becomes obsolete. A real revolution has begun when it becomes clear that women cross the threshold of power not as competitors for that power, or as petitioners, but as people for whom power has a different significance. The shift in significance has been greatly helped by a social change that was brought about partly from the need for both partners in a household to earn and (which is the chicken and which is the egg?) partly by the pressure for change from the women's movements of various kinds. If women have learned not only to cross thresholds to different stages but to interpret differently the significance of those stages, they have been greatly helped by the shift that is happening more and more in the description of the "domestic" stage as one mainly appropriate to women. More couples, mostly middle class but often working class too, share child-care and household chores as they share incomes from the paid work of both partners. The fact that it has become possible for men to take on significant roles on the domestic stage without necessarily experiencing this as humiliating ("women's work") has helped to change the significance of the threshold between public and private life. Men have discovered how much skill and energy it takes to run a home and women have discovered that being a "breadwinner" is not necessarily as liberating or as ego-boosting as it seemed from one side of the domestic threshold. Now, because men and women can share both "stages," shifting from one to the other, it becomes easier to recognize that employment, meaning paid work, is not the only economically significant kind of work.

The process of reimagining that has followed, as well prompting, the shift in self-perception through these shared roles is only in its early stages, if we look at the global scene and even if only the "developed" world is considered, but it is ongoing, inevitable backlash notwithstanding. As an important part of a feminist agenda it has far wider implications than (possibly) easing the lot of women because the partner can cook dinner or bathe the baby. It is a shift that can potentially help to reinvigorate those networks of local self-help for both sexes, which existed before the industrial revolution among women, were reshaped by men in response to the stresses and hardship of industrial life, and are now re-emerging in reaction to centralized capitalistic government and business. But as this blurring of gender roles opens up possibilities, it is important to recognize that the possibilities and the language that can articulate them are the product in some essential ways of women's reflection, reimagining and choices.

It is commonplace to say that the industrial revolution separated home and work. Mothers and children as well as men worked in the mills and factories and mines, but the places and conditions in which they lived outside the workplace were considered irrelevant to their work provided they continued to get themselves to the factory gates at the right time. It is a romantic illusion that pre-industrial home-based work (spinning, weaving, farming, sewing) was necessarily less ill-paid and unhealthy than factory work, but the shape of it did not cut off employment from home life.

It is significant, for instance, that in this pre-industrial period few smaller homes had ovens and almost none had running water. Therefore baking was done in a communal oven and water fetched from the village or neighborhood pump. With few hospitals or doctors for the poor the midwives and nurses were local women without "training" but often with considerable skill, learned from older women and constantly "updated" through experience. In other words interaction between households, and a degree at least of community interdependence, was imposed by necessity, and women were at the heart of this network of local self-help and knew it and taught it to their daughters. Rough and ready as it was, and without disguising or romanticizing (as some nineteenth century artists and novelists did) the hardship and ill-health and ignorance that was built into such a way of life, we can still recognize that what industrialism destroyed was not only the geographical linking of home and employment but the support networks of the poor, and especially of the women. In time, men organized for better wages and conditions and women benefited too, but the organizing (building societies, cooperatives, workmen's colleges) and the resulting changes were male-instigated and male controlled, and in many places there was bitter resentment about women's attempts to organize too, whether at the level of the unions or at the level of government, though women did succeed in organizing unions and leading strikes, especially in industries involving mostly women workers, as in textiles. The separation of home from work was taken for granted by both.

What we are talking about is what has already been the result, for women and for poor people and for all people, of regarding the things that women have done as equally significant for human well-being as those done by men. This does not mean simply acknowledging the immense service that women's activities provide *for* something else—the community, the nation, the future, the war effort, or whatever. It means reimagining the way the human community values, and therefore organizes, its activities, putting things women have done in the middle, on stage, not because of women's rights but for the sake of the community's health. If we start with the things that traditionally happened in the women's spaces, we find that we begin with fundamentals—provision of food, clothing, shelter, health care. These things can then be seen not as something individuals, families or any other groups acquire *from* the wider economy but as things that are generated *by* a human community because it needs them and because it has the skills and the will to grow or build or otherwise create what it needs. Employment ceases to be something you do in order to earn so as to buy what someone else makes available. It becomes what you do as part of a network of many kinds of work that help to keep the community (of whatever size) physically and spiritually healthy, and this is what couples who share both domestic and public roles are discovering. Networks between communities provide for wider exchanges, obviously, but the crucial difference is that the emphasis is on the ability of a given community to know what it needs and how it can work with others to supply those needs. And "needs" include the nurturing of an awareness of human interdependence with all living systems in a scheme of global homemaking.

This reimagining of what "employment" means is of course a vision of alternative economics, and it is necessarily complex, but in practice it can be done and is being done even within the existing system, and the sharing of domestic work has been a significant help in allowing the imaginative shift that makes this possible. My point is that while the urgent need to reimagine employment derived initially in great measure from consideration of women's frustrations, in fact it is not a "feminist" issue in the more usual sense of focusing on women's rights and needs as opposed to those of other human categories. It is, instead, a way to reimagine the relationships between the spaces in which human beings go about their various occupations.

In terms of the house image the whole building that is the place of human habitation has a different feel to it when imagined in this way. For one thing, it is no longer a refuge, it is not just the place to go back to, it is not back stage. It is the focus of living, but when one opens a door and steps out from this important place, the other spaces into which one moves are also places for living, part of the home in some sense. It seems at first that one could say that the walls have become unnecessary, that there is no "public" or "domestic" anymore, but what has really happened is that there are possible choices about what is public and what is domestic, or more accurately about what is our local choice (at different levels of localness) and what is our necessary relationship with other communities, whether human or animal or vegetable. We can choose to live very privately and self-sufficiently, within certain limits, or we can choose to be more obviously and functionally interdependent with other systems, making the methods of that interdependence, in a sense, a description of our employment. These "methods of interdependence" will prove to involve the creation of structures, theories and practices of hospitality, as later chapters will explore.

The house has become a center rather than an enclosure, but if it is to provide what is needed for human living, the building must stand up. It must provide the walls that define and describe and give assurance (I know where I live, who I am). Therefore it still has thresholds; the entrances and exits still have great significance, because thresholds are places where people shift from one mode of being to another. What is done with the spaces on either side of the threshold depends on the way people experience themselves as they make that transition. Are they going "back stage" to wait for another moment of "entrance" or are they making an entrance into another area of different but equal significance? Above all, in terms of the dilemma of Rosencrantz and Guilderstern, are they *choosing* to make the transition, aware of the meaning of the new "acting" area, consciously carrying the drama forward? Or are they shifting from exit to entrance at the whim of unknown forces?

Lucien Kroll, in his book *The Architecture of Complexity,* X warns that "we should be suspicious of nostalgic admiration for beautifully organized spaces conceived at a time that has nothing in common with our era," but he is also aware that nostalgia is an important human experience, reflecting a need to be in touch with community (family, religious, ethnic), and with origins and history. The kind of reflection we have to do concerns the reimagining of spaces in our community structures with a view to providing for the development of public, significant and identity-creating activities that have previously been relegated to the dim though hard-working areas of back stage, or the supportive role of audiences. The questions that arise affect decisions about urban planning, agriculture, architecture (naturally!), education, employment, transport—one can go on and on. But major changes of the kind envisaged by such imaginative shifts depend on a kind of energy that involves vision and creativity but also levels of commitment, endurance and patience that are unusual. For many people, just surviving economically and emotionally takes all their energy, and for many others the "inertia selling" of the status quo ante is so effective that they will only seriously contemplate change when their own situation becomes unbearable. Even then the immediate reaction is often vengeful rather than creative.

The kind of energy that fuels effective change and is yet able to be sensitive to the essential nature of the structures to be changed is the energy we think of as spiritual. The studies of anthropologists as well as psychologists have demonstrated that psychic energy is released in what are called "liminal" states, and *limina* is the Latin word for "threshold." It is in the threshold, the transition, that power is liable to erupt. It is at the point where given expectations break down that newness can happen, for good or ill. We are reminded again of how children avoid treading on the gaps between paving stones because you never know what might break out and grab you if you do. People in search of vision, whether they be Native American or Christian or Buddhist hermits or "sixties-ish" hippies, go into the wilderness to find it because the wilderness is the "in between" place outside normal habitation or civilization, beyond the patterns of human planning. And, as Mary Douglas demonstrated in *Purity and Danger,* people and creatures and places that don't fit the categories into which a given culture organizes its life are viewed as either potently sacred or potently dangerous. We can treat "dirt" or "soil" as useful and even beautiful in the garden and be upset by it in the house, where it is out of place. Homosexuals, homeless people, the mentally ill, evoke reactions of fear and hate because of their "unusual" character: they don't fit and are felt to be dangerous in a way that has nothing to do with any verifiable risk they might pose. (A certain writer whom I haven't been able to identify was reported to have declared that "sodomy caused earthquakes" and was believed, at least by some.) But other people who don't fit, people who may wear strange clothes, speak unknown languages or claim unique information, can be revered as saints and treated as sources of ultimate wisdom.

Power is in the thresholds. Apparently random and unpredictable as this power may be, we need it. Without it nothing changes—and without it what does not change cannot endure either. Mysteriously, the thresholds are the places of power, for the preservation of the human building and for its changing.

6

Permeability

*I*n the previous chapter I attempted to explore the symbolism of thresholds in terms of the stage image, which "Ros and Guil" explodes rather effectively, forcing us to ask disturbing questions about our normal assumptions of where significance lives—where the "stage" is. These questions have to do with the meanings of passage from one state to another in emotional social, economic and political change and development. But I suggested that the energy that makes transitions possible is not contained in the spaces to which they give access, but in the liminal experience itself. We are then in the area of the strange and by definition "indefinite"!

This strangeness has turned out to be an integral part of the very practical need to reimagine the human home, because reimagining depends on clear information about the what and how of the structure and a freedom to shift how we perceive it. That involves such strange expedients as experiencing fantasy while rooted in the every day, exploring forgotten and forbidden cellars and crossing into new spaces of mind and body. So this chapter engages more precisely with that strangeness and the particular and life-giving kind of anachronism that we think of as spiritual. This kind of spirituality, far from being separated from material reality, depends on it. This shift from one mode of perception to another is encountered, not merely observed; it requires choices and actions; it requires that we cross the thresholds, braving the liminal dragons.

Human attempts to deal with these dangerous, powerful and essential thresholds are in the realms of what is referred to as "religious." This word has many different meanings and evokes all kinds of different emotions, positive or negative. It is, however, the only one that is accurate. For my purpose I take "religion" to mean the systems of thought and behavior by that human beings try to deal with those areas of their lives that are at least in some measure beyond their understanding or control, and yet which are certainly important: death, birth, "luck," the fact of existence as opposed to non-existence, and experiences of a mystical, magical or otherwise "non-fitting" nature.

The entrance to the "stage" where imaginatively powerful events occur has a mystique about it that is religious in character. Ros and Guil, pushed around by a power they try frantically to interpret, find themselves on stage in a drama they only marginally understand, and their fear is a religious fear, superstition seeking a basis in reality, gazing over the edge into depths of significance that are too awe-ful to contemplate. They want boundaries and constantly lack them. Their need to be on stage, yet their fear that the real action is actually somewhere else and controlled by others, underlies much of what I have been describing, in terms of the attempt to make an imaginative switch, to redefine the nature of the place where I find myself and to discover an ability to act effectively even in other spaces in which I am not "at home."

In Bristol, in southwest England, there is a big Victorian church which, like many others, at a certain point found that its congregation was too small either to fill the space or pay for its upkeep. The solution chosen in this case was not to pull down and rebuild, or to sell the space for other uses, but to lift the floor of the worship area halfway up to the high gothic vault, creating a space underneath which became a nursery school and offices. The new worship area brought the congregation up near the vaulted ceiling, the top half of the columns and their great arches springing immediately into the traceries of the roof. The implications of such a change have to do with a switch in imagining sacred space. Providing space for the education of children within a sacred building (in ways not specifically religious such as a Sunday school) challenges people to be aware that what goes on in a nursery has its own kind of sacredness. This is different from building various spaces for human services (day-care, hospital, school) that are funded by a church. These may "belong" to the church but they are "back stage" from the "religious" point of view if religion is thought of as primarily to do with cult or ritual. One exits from the sacred space into the area of the non-sacred, including homes. But in this Bristol church the nature of the worship experience is itself subtly changed because what goes on in this gothic space can no longer be the only sacred action. The entrance to the worship space is up stairs that ascend over the entrance to the children's space, and the nearness to the vault, not far above the worshipers' heads, helps to nurture a different consciousness of the nature of ritual and the significance of the thresholds between sacred and secular. "Up there," under the clearly seen roof that was once so remote and mysterious, the pervasive dualism of traditional Christianity is constantly challenged. "High" and "low" change their feeling. By this simple change of space the image of God is changed, and so the nature of worship, because we are "high" too, and because below, in the same building, the work of caring for children is going on and asserts its validity as a godly act. The layout of altar, lectern, benches in the worship space is familiar but the change is real and irreversible, though probably not much consciously considered.

In Jewish households the whole cycle of year-round ritual is in fact based in the home, with synagogue worship as a support to that. The synagogue or temple is a place of religious study and community affirmation, but without the long-lost focus of the temple in Jerusalem the religious life of the people is centered in homes, and detailed observance—daily, weekly and seasonal—assumes a consciousness of the home itself as the place where God is known and worshiped. Sacred space, then, is not a separate physical area but something that is specifically affirmed at certain times and in certain ways, within the same living space. Special dishes, candlesticks, clothing, are brought out, and thus the stage is defined, the time and place for the significant action separated, the actors prepared for their entrances. This is not like the apron-off dinner-party ritual, which tries temporarily (and half for fun) to "forget" the everyday reality of the same space. The sabbath ritual, for instance, does not "forget" the weekday family meals at the same table; rather it sanctifies them. Food and drink—all food and drink—are in some way sacramentalized.

To use the word *sacrament* in connection with a Jewish ritual is perhaps a theological anachronism, but anachronism is one of the important elements in making possible the switches of awareness that are needed to deal with change without disaster. The words *sacrament* and *sacramentality* indicate a way of thinking that has shaped ritual and religion in the west, and which is an essential pointer to a way in which the house we live in has to be understood. We can give to the spaces of living a religious and ritual significance, and we give it to objects and people too, in that context. The church with a nursery school inside it, the Jewish house rituals, are about how to allow people to make contact with divine power, aweful and even dangerous as it is, in ways that are safe and realistic. Even religious groups that emphasize ecstatic states and mystical experience provide specific places and times for these things to happen; when such things are done without properly defined physical or ritual structures designed for them—for instance in some cases of exorcism or certain kinds of charismatic leadership with no built-in accountability—the results can be lethal.

Our difficulty is to discover how spiritual energy may be made available in a culture whose house includes would-be sacred spaces that don't feel sacred anymore, or are the wrong shape or in the wrong place, and also a culture in that the most used and, from one point of view, obviously important spaces may lack real spiritual significance. St. Paul's Cathedral in London, for instance, is one of many religious buildings which, beautiful and uplifting aesthetically as they may be, have become more of a museum and a "sight" than places where the beholder might experience the numinous.

Anachronism is once more a helpful key idea, and as always a disturbing one.

The "chronos" in this ana-chronism is the need that human beings have to make sense of their lives by creating ritual patterns, demarcations, spaces, entrances, exits, definitions of significance. A concept cannot be thought unless it can be expressed in words, and one language can make it possible to *think* something that is literally unthinkable in another language. In the same way ritual is how we affirm significance in our lives, and the things we are able to affirm as significant vary. Things omitted from the ritual are excluded from significance.

In Jewish ritual there is a clear signification of food, home, family, in relation to a notion of God and of the people of Israel. "The people" is the point of encounter with God, and so all that sustains the life of the people as a distinct entity must be clearly signified as part of that relation. The signification is constantly repeated, in exactly the same form, so the connections are entwined with all of life that is included in the significance. Business and working life are not specifically signified, and although they will be affected by the moral values and decisions of the good person, they are not ritualized. They are back stage in relation to this ritual action.

Rituals and thresholds of the corporate world—who has which office, who makes the coffee, what is appropriate clothing and what kinds of considerations are appropriately introduced into decision making—also make clear where the significant action is, and exactly where are the exits, beyond which behavior is not observed and in a sense does not exist. Yet businesses are aware that it is actually dangerous to ignore what goes on "back stage." If employees' "back stage" lives are disrupted, it can affect their work "on stage"; hence there are such apparently humanitarian arrangements as child-care facilities, maternity leave, and other efforts to ensure that what is not on stage still supports the action. Ritually, such things as office parties to which spouses are invited (rather like the Boxing Day ball for the servants in England a century ago) bestow significance on those whose support is essential, and help to keep them positively engaged.

All this, and most of what goes on in churches of many kinds, is part of the "chronos," the ritualizing, that bestows significance. In Christian churches of the Catholic tradition many of the rituals are theologically described as being sacramental, which means that a special sacred significance is consciously bestowed on certain physical things: bread and wine, oil, water, the bodies of man and woman in marriage. This sacramental idea extends beyond what are strictly known as "sacraments" to include the blessing and sanctifying of fields, candles, ashes, fishing boats, animals, veils, rings, buildings and much more. Without exploring in depth the theology of sacrament the basic idea is that by making use of these things, specifically designated as loci of divine blessing, human beings experience spiritual power in appropriate ways. The ashes that mark the foreheads of the faithful on Ash Wednesday signify mortality, and help in the purification of everyday life by relating it to the certainty of death and the hope of heaven. The "veil" covers a consecrated life, to make a "tent" in which to dwell with God, and at Orthodox weddings bride and groom are both veiled. The fields blessed at Rogationtide, the wheat and vegetables in the churches at the harvest festival and the eucharistic bread itself are all part of the affirmation of divine presence in the production of human food from the earth. In ancient goddess religions the womb-shaped grave symbolized the significance of death as a return to the mother for rebirth.

The sacramental idea makes specific connections between God and human beings by way of definite material things, including human bodies. Thus these things are marked out as significant, as part of the drama of divine dealings with the world. At its best, this tradition is a rich affirmation of the goodness of creation, bringing daily lives into the space of divine action by clear signification.

The weakness of sacramental thinking as a guide to ritual behavior is that it can easily become so specific that it makes it possible for most of daily life to be left out. The accumulation of eucharistic and sacramental theology over the centuries of Christian religion, most of it in the Catholic and Orthodox traditions (including Anglican) and developed in the interests of keeping the sacramental rituals as a clerical preserve, has increasingly limited the scope of symbolic significance. More and more, sacramentality became something that happened in church, was done by certain people only, in certain ways at certain times for very specific spiritual purposes. The connection between eucharistic bread and bread on the family table was minimized, and if you wanted holy water you brought it home from a church in a bottle. Efforts have been made in recent years to redress this and to open up the area of sacredness, but with limited success. Books and lectures and liturgies created by a theological elite who talk mostly to each other, however eloquently, have not undone the destructive work of the past.

alas, true!

The Protestant tradition, while less clerical, minimized sacramentality because of its perceived tendency toward idolatry (that is, the actual location of the divine in material things) in favor of emphasizing the presence of the divine in the heart of the believer and the possibility of unmediated access to God. This was liberating, and created the possibility of the ordinary as locus of the divine immanence in uncategorized spaces and people and things. By this path a new value for sacramentality was eventually discovered, but for both traditions it was too late, too cerebral and conscious. At some point a spirituality that could be at the heart of everyday life without conscious personal effort was found to be not there.

Many people in search of spiritual sense are, in consequence, walking away from churches, or trying to stake out a survival area within a religious structure that has become largely meaningless to them. They continue to do this because every now and then their church experience opens a cupboard door, or catches a view through a cobwebby window, or explores a neglected attic, and finds treasures. And the treasure can't be taken out; it belongs there. Somehow there is a space for the spirit, though it may seem to be a narrow one. They cling to the religious chronos because of its ability, somehow, to give way to the anachronism that is divine, but that clinging can itself reveal an experience of anachronism that does not depend on arranged sacred spaces and yet is linked to them.

Anachronism doesn't mean anything without chronos, but chronos is in itself incapable of alteration. It just goes on. Change happens in the real human experience of time because there is a lot more to time than succession of minutes and years. Ritual can sanctify chronos, sacramentality makes succession spiritually significant, but it can only do so because anachronism keeps popping out of the thresholds of succession and making them ludicrous, frightening, awesome and essentially comforting. Anachronism has to do with the switch of imagination when an exit from the sacred stage we've been taught to recognize turns out to be an entrance into the spaces of the spirit, a mystery from which sacredness springs.

Here we move into a region where words begin to get out of control, yet only when they do (but not so far we can't catch them and dance with them) can we get a glimpse of exits that are entrances.

Time, succession, and the structures we create to ensure that we can go on living in time threaten us with the sudden discovery that, like "Ros and Guil," we are in a play we can't understand, and we don't even know where the stage is. The glimpses of sense then turn out to be senseless (like betting with a tossed coin that *always* comes up heads) and empty out the significance we thought we had. We open a door that had seemed solid, but when we go through it we see it was only a stage door, and when we look back there's no stage. Time as significant is emptied out; only what is "obvious" remains, and it turns out not to be obvious at all. There is an aching need for an unattainable kind of knowledge beyond chronos, something that has to do with the thresholds, the exits and entrances during which we are neither on stage nor off, in a non-space, non-time charged with the significance without which space, time, chronos, are horribly empty.

But all the same we are afraid to be left in that non-space and non-time. We need the rhythms, the cycles of seasons and lives to feel safe. Within them we can safely (or fairly safely) face those liminal experiences. These are what religion has always tried to supply, for without them we encounter the horrible fear experienced by Guil early in the play when he tries to put together the memories of an urgent summons, of a game with the coin that defies all laws of probability, with a realization that they don't even know which way they are supposed to go:

Guil: We better get on.
Ros: Right! (Pause) On where?
Guil: Forward.
Ros: Ah...which way do we...which way did we...?
Guil: Practically starting from scratch...An awakening, a man standing on his saddle to bang on the shutters, our names shouted in a certain dawn, a message, a summons....A new record for heads and tails. We have not been...picked out simply to be abandoned...set loose to find our way....We are entitled to some direction, I would have thought.

Ros and Guil suffer an indecision that is not outside them but is the essence of the situation. They long for a direction, a sense of who, and where, they are. Their tragedy is that they never do find out, and the excruciating and very funny experience of watching the play is due to the accuracy with which Stoppard has expressed the basic human experience of knowing there must be meaning, knowing it is only just out of sight, but never quite catching it. Ros and Guil live on the edge where chronos breaks down into anachronism, but it seems as if the relationship between the two, which it is the business of religion crazily to explore, is always happening somewhere else.

Sacred space is delineated by ritual, but many rituals (like those of the office or the restaurant) are virtually free from anachronism except that, of course, when viewed with detachment by those not involved, they are so "unreal" that their solid chronos quality is itself a kind of anachronism. Ritual can indeed delineate sacred space, but it cannot by itself offer an encounter with that which gives it sacredness. The knowledge that is indicated is not attainable, yet it works; it is what goes on, somewhere, somehow. It is only when the ache of the space where knowledge should be is accepted, the indecision suffered with intention (as Ros and Guil could not, so in the end they just ceased) that the human spirit can find a home, a space of the spirit, within the rhythm and the return of the seasons.

There is a helpful illustration of how this religious/dramatic experience of anachronism can actually be *prevented* from happening, with excellent intentions, in considering what happened to the play *Rosencranz and Guilderstern Are Dead* when it was transferred to film. It certainly became much easier, technically, for the film makers than for the stage director to create those drastic shifts by which the two friends are at one moment in a wood tossing a coin and the next in the palace of Elsinor, at one moment "themselves" (whatever that is) and at another maybe two quite different people. But in fact the mind-jolting effect of "every exit being an entrance somewhere else" is to some extent lost precisely because the camera can make those visual shifts so easily. The people in the audience don't have to drag their perception across gaping holes in the reality presented in order to keep up with the action. The camera does it for them; there is no struggle, no paradox, therefore no illumination and no humor: not that the film is humorless, or unilluminating, but these qualities depend, much more than in the stage play, on the ability of the actors to create the *effect* of having themselves experienced these wrenching transitions. We, the audience, need to experience the effort and the pain of making those switches for them to be spiritually liberating.

In the last half century some churches became aware that in much traditional religious ritual the ancient symbols had lost a great deal of their meaning. In attempting to make the symbols more accessible to contemporary people the ritual and its symbols were simplified, translated, explained. The result often seems pre-digested and bland, unchallenging even if beautifully done, though the continuity of very ancient human symbols cannot fail to keep some of its essential power in word, music, gesture, gift. In the Roman Catholic tradition the power of the most universal symbols has indeed somehow been liberated by reformed liturgy. The action of breaking out sudden light in the darkened church at Easter, for instance, stirs the deep and ancient pools of awareness that were discussed in Chapter 4, however perfunctory the performance of the ritual.

This desire to make ritual accessible in the Catholic tradition has led, in some cases, to a return to some very early forms of ritual, for instance the celebration of eucharist with the priest facing the people, as in the early basilican churches. But what this did was to move the real questions further back. When the action of the breaking and blessing of bread became fully visible, then the kind of sacramental theology built up through centuries when (and in some cases possibly *because*) this act was remote and quasi-invisible at the end of a long narrow church and hidden by the priest's back, itself lost credibility. The questions raised by the sacramental symbol were changed, and not answered. The substitution of "warm fuzzies" (togetherness, cheerful hymns, banners) for mystical indicators left many with a sense of loss, without exactly knowing what was lost. Much was often gained in the sense of community and responsibility in a local church; the losses were in the area of sacramental—that is, liminal—awareness.

Where is the sacred space in the human house of the future? How can we create a sacramentality (time-sensitive, based in the physical, comfortable in appropriate spaces) that allows the creative disruption of anachronism? How does the experience of sacred space translate into spaces of the spirit in all the structures of living?

Two very different experiences offer a way to identify the ancient sacred space in the new spaces of the spirit. One has to do with the refusal to be distracted by concerns about sacred places and people and things, an attempt to live with chronos and anachronism as equal daily companions, trying to establish the shifting vision as a conscious spiritual discipline, at least in principle. The other does almost the opposite—pushing the external symbol, the principle of sacramentality, to its furthest and most dramatic point, so that the essential anachronistic dependence on something other is unavoidable.

The first experience is the great Quaker tradition. In the seventeenth century, England was not only torn by civil war but experiencing the aftermath of a century of religious uncertainty, when the collapse of papal rule under Henry VIII and its brief reimposition under Mary Tudor left a legacy of doctrinal and liturgical confusion, and the imposition of a reformed faith combined with the maintenance of a reduced but important sacramental system under Elizabeth and James created a situation in which ordinary people did not know whom or what to believe and clergy were placed and displaced and replaced with bewildering speed. George Fox was one of many who experienced the emptying of sacramental (that is, God-encountering) value from the places and rituals of the formal religion that finally entrenched itself. The newly "established" Anglican church was, in fact, going through much genuine and agonizing self-criticism and a search for what could be affirmed as its genuine expression. It was inspiring people such as George Herbert, and Nicholas Ferrar and his lay community at Little Gidding. But the experience of many ordinary parishes was of a parson with much concern for the local landlord (to whom he owed his living) and very little for the spiritual needs of his flock. Many of these men had been appointed more with a view to excluding Puritans or "Papists" than for their level of dedication. It was in the spiritual void created by such experiences that many informal and enthusiastic sects erupted. One, already referred to, was the very small but recently much studied sect called the "Diggers" because of its communistic lifestyle in which members claimed that all land was common human property, under God, and demonstrated this by taking over "waste" land and digging and planting in it. They claimed the authority of the gospel, had no clergy, and refused to pay rent. Needless to say, even Cromwell's "Commonwealth" (which was just as much run by land owners as the monarchic system) could not stand for such doctrines and behavior and their small settlements were wiped out.

George Fox got away with more because he did not claim land or property. Rather he claimed the freedom of each man or woman to experience the grace of God directly and powerfully without benefit of clergy and without the need for "steeple houses," as he called the church buildings. His enemies were, naturally, the clergy as well as the landlords who had appointed those clergy to keep the common people in dutiful subjection. George was often beaten and imprisoned for preaching in churchyards and for popping up in churches during services to denounce what he saw as empty rituals and false clerical claims. He preached that there was "that of God" in each person so that when people gathered for worship anywhere, anytime, the Spirit was among them and inspiring them.

The doctrine spread rapidly among people hungry for meaning and hope in a chaotic and oppressive political situation, when powerful people fought for ownership of the land but nobody—least of all, apparently, the church—cared what happened to those who actually lived on and by it.

It was one of George Fox's converts, a landowner's wife called Margaret Fell, who gave shape and organization to George's movement for spiritual freedom. Without her it seems likely that it would have remained a matter of spontaneous local gatherings arising in the wake of George's erratic mission. Possibly this is what he would actually have preferred, but he himself was caught up in the spread of a reality that increasingly had a visible corporate identity and therefore a need to be able to state its beliefs. Eventually, after her husband's death, Margaret married George, though the demands of the growing Society of Friends, as it struggled with persecution, emigration and the organizational tangle of local groups, meant that they didn't actually spend much time together.

The story is amazing and complex. The outcome of the combination of George's uncompromising commitment to a spirit-led egalitarian assembly and Margaret's talent for organization was actually a unique process of institutionalizing something that contradicted all the expected and normal structures of institutions. It was non-hierarchical, it was gender-blind (a particular source of public outrage), it had no center of government, no person or group to decide what the Society did or did not believe. Yet it "grew" a method of what would now be called "networking." It (or rather Margaret) devised ways to keep local meetings in touch with each other through regional and national meetings which, with modifications, still endure. Conflict about belief and behavior could be gradually worked out, not without pain and turmoil, but without resort (at least until much later) to either schism or heresy hunts.

The importance of this experience for my purposes lies in this strange combination of essential spiritual freedom and spontaneity within a structure that protects the possibility of that freedom and spontaneity. Friends do not acknowledge the need for a sacred space, or for any sacred ritual or symbol system. There are no "sacraments" in Quaker worship. The celebration of marriage, and the missioning of a minister to go and carry the message, are by simple assertion. There are no presiding ministers, for all minister to one another. (In some United States Quaker traditions, however, there are now, in fact, appointed permanent ministers, and rows of pews face the pulpit from which he presides.)

This refusal to acknowledge that the inherence of divine presence and power be located only in particular people, places, objects or gestures means that Friends must discern the divine ("that of God") in each person and in every place or thing. This is a very difficult thing to do, in effect demanding a level of mystical awareness that is hard to maintain even by the mystically gifted and bordering on the impossible for more distracted mortals. In practice, therefore, the belief is made bearable and manageable by the availability of regularized meetings.

At these the shared, common conviction of the presence of divine power helps the individual to "center" and become aware of the Spirit, even though people can be "in meeting" in twos or threes, at any time or place, as well as at regular weekly times. Such regular meetings are not rituals in any obvious sense, but they concretize the ongoing possibility of divine encounter by locating it in space and time. They pinpoint the inherent but diffused sacredness in all things and times. They indicate that possibly what is needed in the search for spaces of the spirit in the religious context but also in others is to work at the elusive connection between overtly sacred symbols and the aspects of everyday life to which they refer.

The traditional Quaker Meeting House, for instance is intended to be merely a convenient and pleasant space in which Friends gather and where they can be open to the unlocalized spirit. But just by virtue of its use for this purpose, and by the continuity of its use, the place acquires a significance that is beyond the purely everyday. It speaks of faith, and brotherly and sisterly love and sharing; it expresses the beliefs that dictate its form (no altar, but benches facing one another) and its use. This immediately throws light on the way in which we need to think about other human spaces. If a Quaker Meeting House expresses a conviction about the availability of the Spirit in the gathered congregation, it does so on the basis of the belief that the spirit is available anywhere.

Yet if a "meeting" can take place anywhere, then that "anywhere" should somehow *also* imply, by the way it is built, (and lit, furnished, entered) the constant possibility of divine epiphany. Kitchens, factories, board rooms, planning offices, hospital wards, are all places where (so the Meeting House witnesses) the Spirit can descend on the gathered people. Therefore, the way *any* place is built should reflect this ongoing reality; its design should express those values of respect and trust on which such common spiritual experience depends.

The implication is that, while we do not need to exit the "insignificant" spaces of everyday and enter the "stage" of an assigned sacred space in order to experience the power of the spirit, the existence of a space where that experience is specifically sought helps us to recognize the sacredness of those other spaces and build them and use them accordingly. The early Quakers revolted against the organization of a claimed sacredness that seemed to empty out the possibility of actual sacredness. Their experience and practice helps us to recognize a need for visible, available, symbolic statements about the nature of sacredness as a human context.

In the nineteenth century, the Anglo-Catholic revival inspired priests and laity to raise funds to build large, richly decorated gothic churches in the middle of the devastating poverty of the new industrial slums. On the face of it, given the stark absence of necessities, from food and decent homes to midwifery services and schools, this enthusiasm for building expensive churches can seem to reflect a dualism that separates spiritual needs from material ones to the neglect of the material. In fact, such schemes grew from a wholistic vision of human life (though the builders wouldn't have used such a word) that affirmed the spiritual dignity of even the poorest and their right to an experience of the sacred equal to that of the wealthier and better educated. They built schools and hospitals too, and created sisterhoods and "settlements" of various kinds to run clinics, girls' clubs and other services. Not all were offered in a way that fully affirmed the equal dignity of the poor because the insight that brought ritual beauty into the inner city could not fully overcome class prejudice and ignorance, but their achievements were heroic, and worthy of study by their spiritual descendants who are wrestling with even worse and more intransigent social ills.

The hope of the creators of splendid space and rituals in such degraded surroundings was that (to use the terms of my discussion) the experience of entering onto the stage of the sacred, the space where fundamentally significant events are enacted, would have the effect that I suggested in connection with revaluating women's spaces: the worshipers would discover, through the ritual experience, a way to make an imaginative shift in viewing their own everyday, squalid situations. They would not afterward simply exit into the back stage, the non-life of the slums where people are "not real" in terms of the concerns of "real" people. They would learn instead to "enter" onto the other stage of their lives, now become significant and therefore capable of real drama, leading to real change in which they themselves could take part.

In practice, this did not happen in the way hoped for, partly because many poor people in England continued to regard the Anglican churches as places for the middle classes (the poor, if they wanted to worship, were more likely to go to Methodist chapels or, if Irish, to the new Roman Catholic churches) and partly because if they were attracted and wanted to get involved in church initiatives for social change they could only do so as subordinate helpers in a system set up for, not with, them by their "betters"; such situations did not encourage initiative or facilitate transformative experience. At that time, the growing trade unions and the self-help movements of co-ops and friendly societies were the real grassroots organizing in town, and their members rarely felt at home in elaborate neo-gothic ecclesiastical setups.

But the vision was there, and it was valid. It provides a kind of extra comment on the insight developed in the context of Quaker worship, that sacred space (and the roles and events involved) offer a true encounter with the sacred if the consciously ritual context is experienced as a validation of the equal sacredness of other, non-ritual, human contexts. This is important because when the sacred space is separated off as the single appropriate stage for the divine-human encounter it loses its power, precisely as sacred. If the power of the gods and goddesses is only known as real within the ritual areas, then it can be evaded or ignored outside that context. This is as damaging to the official minister as to the laity. People with valuable ritual roles whose own identity is wrapped up in their roles are easily tempted to seek to preserve their monopoly on the sacred by the creation of guilt in the laity over moral or ritual lapses or by making religious conformity the badge of social acceptability, and this bestows power and prestige, since clergy claim to be the only judges of spiritual validity. None of this fosters sacramental awareness—that is, the consciousness of the sacred as a quality of life, illumined by, but not confined to, specific ritual events and spaces. All religious establishments of which I have any knowledge (my knowledge is, however, far from comprehensive) use this kind of manipulation to maintain authority, whether we are talking of the priests and Levites of the time of Jesus, clergy in the Catholic tradition (Roman or Anglican or Orthodox), Jewish rabbis, evangelical preachers or Islamic fundamentalist leaders, though in all these and many other religious elites there are many, also, who use their role to empower and liberate.

In the end, religious manipulation doesn't work. People escape into other religions or no religion, or into indifference or mysticism. They may "cheat," just keeping quiet about moral decisions that are not acceptable to the religious authorities, (as many Roman couples use birth control without a qualm) because they still value the religious observance in which they continue to hope that the sacredness they were promised can be found. If not now, then later—after death, perhaps?

If the right use of sacred structures (spaces, rituals, symbols, roles) is to illustrate the sacramental nature of life in other contexts, so that the exit from the stage of sacred action is an entrance to another sacramental stage, then the way in which the overtly sacred is displayed is clearly of basic importance. This includes structures (material or organizational or mental) such as those of Quaker organization and worship spaces, whose stated purpose is to avoid specifically sacred character. It has to do with the way, also mentioned earlier, in which Jewish households hold celebrations to express the sacredness not so much of the place and the individuals present as of the people as a whole, as God's people, whose whole way of life is designed to show that they are in fact engaged in the sacred drama to which they are called.

The risk, in structures that avoid the localizing of the sacred, is that sacramentality will be so diffused that it is never recognized. The opposite risk, that of ritualistic religious practice, is that sacramentality becomes so localized as to be (no matter what the theologian says) in practice virtually unavailable anywhere but in the sacred location and in the hands of sacred personnel.

A way to discover a possible alternative understanding rather than a middle ground can be explored through the second of the two experiences that, I suggested, may show a way to locate (in the sense of "find" and in the sense of "put") sacred space in the changing habitation of the human spirit, and create spaces of the spirit.

A picture by David Jones, painted in 1943 and entitled "A Latere Dextro," offers a very good definition of the nature of the challenge. This title is part of a quotation from the prophet Ezekiel's vision of the new temple, in which he saw water flowing "from the right side" of the temple under the altar, and becoming a great river of life on whose banks grew trees for food and healing. The phrase became part of the Catholic liturgical offices for Good Friday, and was used to refer to the water which, in the gospel of John, flows from the right side of the dead Christ and is a symbol of the work of cleansing and regeneration wrought by his sacrifice.

In this complex, fantastic and delicate water-color drawing, a priest saying mass raises the chalice of Christ's blood. Under a small altar to one side is a carved relief of the paschal lamb, which is wounded, and blood flows from its side, into a chalice and thence into a pool that at that point escapes the carved semblance and truly flows. On a pedestal on the other side a statue of Mary, the mother of God, who is also the grail (vessel of divine vision), holds up the body of her dead son. Little acolytes in white surplices carry the censer, lift the priest's vestment as he raises his arms, and ring the bell, while two others hold candles, and beside them an iron stand holds up yet more candles. Between two springing arches of the chapel the legendary Pelican broods in carving over her young, piercing her breast so that blood may flow to feed them.

There is nothing new or unusual in this gathering of sacred symbols. They are ancient, and instantly recognizable in the context of Christian iconography, while they have their roots in pre-Christian symbolism also. But in this painting the intertwined and traditional symbols are literally blown away, for a gale of wind billows the vestments into great banners, drags the candle flames into long smoking curves and makes the candles burn so rapidly that they keel over, half melted by their own heat. The carved Madonna's hair streams in the wind from under her crown, altar curtains become sails on a ship, and the air is filled with cascades of delicate, many-colored flowers. The carved doves on the capitals of the pillars kiss one another and seem about to fly away. As for the priest, as he lifts his arms light streams from wounds in his hands and feet and side.

In this evocation, we enter an ancient and traditional space with its old stone columns and its altars, used routinely decade after pious decade in rhythms of religion and the succession of the seasons, and find that it is also the place where the power to which it has been for the most part routinely and unthinkingly dedicated suddenly takes over, changing everything, and yet in the change making all of it more clearly itself. Old myths of sacrifice and regeneration become immediate, the boundary between reality and representation (the statue's blown hair, the blood that flows away from a carved cup) and earth's flowers whirl through it all in a wild dance with the candle flames, while wide-eyed children are swept up beyond their understanding.

This picture somehow makes the "chronos" of religion permeable, anachronistic in the sense that things can't be counted on to behave in predictable ways. The actors in Stoppard's play thought they were acting in one play and found themselves in a different and unimaginably different one, which still had the same cast and the same props. At the same time they became audience to another play that seemed to be going on round and through them. The actors in David Jones' other and sacred drama are also other than themselves, and yet their own time-and-space-bound eyes are necessary if this play of divine presence is to be performed. As the Player says, "We're *actors*...we pledged our identities, secure in the convention of our trade, that someone would be watching."

A drama—even a sacred drama—can only happen if it has an audience, but the audience to such a drama can never be only an audience; it must also be playing its own play and discovering its own reality, because of the drama in which its role is that of spectator. Spiritual truth requires that two plays—material/earthy and symbolic—coincide in the same space, distinct dramas, neither of which can have meaning without the other. The priest in David Jones' picture is spectator of a sacrifice and a drama whose origins are before history, but (and he needs both to know and not know this) he is also the actor in that drama; he is the victim, the dead and arising god, John Barleycorn, Osiris, Christ. He is the bleeding lamb, source of the water of life, but only if he is also audience to that cosmic action, giving it validity by observing it, or (at another point) stage-hand, ensuring the working of an illusion that is necessary if reality is to be perceived at all.

The little boys are little boys, going on doing what they have learned to do, actors whose well-learned routines are suddenly blown upon by the gale of transforming power so that they become spectators of something else; the carved Lady on her pedestal clutches her dead Child, and watches them, as the wind blows her long hair out of the chronos of stone that cannot deal with such power. She is a prop to their play, while they are essential stage-hands in hers. And the wind that blows between the spaces and times of chronos ensures that there is no confusion, but only that impossible gap in which—and in which alone—sacrament breaks out into sacred.

Words run out of power, the light goes out, we grope around for a match to relight the candles. In their wavering light, and in the light of the sabbath candle, or in the calming air of the Quaker meeting, what can we understand about those other spaces from which the energy needed to live in any space is derived?

First of all we realize that the sacred spaces need not be separate from other living spaces, in physical fact. The cathedral, the temple, the mosque, the monastic church or chapel, can be indeed the sources of sacred energy. (Their thresholds may serve as frames for magic casements, certainly, but those can be found elsewhere.) This applies also to ritual acts and words, for their efficacy as points of anachronistic breakthrough does not totally depend on their uniqueness as gesture or phrase. One can say "I forgive you" in one's own name or God's, and the ancient ritual gesture of fealty to a feudal lord (probably it only happens at British coronations nowadays) is the same as a certain kind of warm handclasp of greeting. What matters is the way in which a recognition is created that the chronos has broken down, the ambiguity of stage, audience and back stage are forcing those imaginative shifts in which spiritual power is apprehended.

David Jones himself wrote about this, expressing in words what he also tried to express in paint. He wrote of the "thickness" of an object (a jug, a table) as having its own magic and its own connections. He was very aware of the elusive and disturbing results of this sacramental threshold. In 1928 he wrote, "It is about how everything turns into something else, and how you can never tell when...the Holy Ghost is going to turn something inside out, and how everything is a balls-up and a kind of 'Praise' at the same time." In 1950 he returns to this theme of the coincidence of realities that cannot be simplified without reducing their meaning, and he saw art—of words or paint or sound—as the guardian of truth. "The arts abhor any loppings off of meanings or emptyings out, any lessening of the totality of connotation, any loss of recession and 'thickness through.'" David Jones tried to push the reader or observer who is, of course, audience and therefore also "actor," to the point of anachronism at which he or she would be forced to encounter sacredness in the sacramental point.

Places are also included in the "objects" that have "thickness through." The places of sacredness (caves, mountains, rivers, buildings, stone circles, the family table on sabbath eve) and also times (Sunday morning, Monday, Friday, or Saturday evening, winter solstice, July fourth or fourteenth, Ramadan, Lent) though they belong with everyday successions have always indicated the possibility at least of an exit that is an entrance into the totally other, the place/time where the real things happen.

If we are imagining or redesigning or repairing our human habitation we have to be aware of this. It is true that if those who design the structures of our world choose to ignore the danger and power of these transitions, life still goes on, at least for a while, though the kind of habitation that is created in such ignorance is now showing distinct signs of impending catastrophe. Meanwhile people find ways to compensate, seeking even unconsciously to repair the damage. Children create their magic circles, light their magic fires and invent their incantations when grown-ups are not looking. Quiet rebels devise a secret language of spiritual subversion, and mystics and visionaries and prophets know better than the power holders, at the risk of ending up in mental hospitals. But for a healing and conceivably healthy habitation these things must not be done only in secret or in opposition. The "kind of integrity" required for sacred action is not that of a system, a universal one-stage play, in which everyone has to take part at their peril. Without respect for the "kind of integrity" and awareness of its possibility the design of the house will provide something more like a prison or a department store than a home.

There is a word used by Lucien Kroll in his *The Architecture of Complexity* that he calls a "third way" in architecture. All the ways are, he says, "political attitudes" and the first "way" is "'centralization' which 'dominates' the sphere of operation, transforming it according to a preconceived image...the ordering system which determines the built form gets projected out to take possession of the environment beyond." An example of this might be the work of the seventeenth century architect Vanbrugh, creating sprawling, gilded palaces and formal gardens to express a philosophy, a triumphant vision, rather than to make a liveable environment. The second way is "objectification," which is "a kind of parking mentality, a tendency to arrange things is rows. The objectivist does not dress up the landscape in his own image like the centralist, indeed he rejects it, detaches himself from it...reduces it to an abstraction, or...a commodity or spectacle. He is ruled by economic considerations...." Such builders created the rows of identical industrial cottages and now create neighborhoods for the poor—and sometimes the rich— according to the predominant architectural fad of the time. Both of these "ways" express "political attitudes" that define exactly where the stage is. They are very different, and the "centralist" has created such masterpieces as Versailles and St. Peter's in Rome, but neither could consider that their exits may be entrances anywhere else at all, and their windows are definitely not "magic casements," and would make it hard to cut any.

Kroll's word for his alternative "third way" is *permeability*. What he says about this is very important because it suggests how the ambiguities of exits and entrances, of chronos and anachronism, of the need for the sacred and for allowing the sacred to relate to (affect and be affected by) the other spaces of living, can actually and practically be accommodated within a comprehensible and habitable human structure. "Permeability" means "seeking out and responding to the special condition of the chosen site," in which "it should prove possible to discover a basis for organization...." Note that "organization" in Kroll's view is different from the "domination" of centrism or the exploitative and what he calls "autistic" character of objectivism. Permeability "can encompass opposites and allow contradictions, but it permits no apathetic indifference...it remains open to the influence of local history and geography," including, naturally, sacred caves, springs or ruins. "At best it *takes root* in such considerations, becoming a natural process, almost a biology."

One of the "centrists" Kroll refers to is, not surprisingly, Le Corbusier. When a group of modernist architects got together to write themselves a charter for architecture, Le Corbusier himself rewrote it to, as he put it, "purify it more completely of all reference to tradition, all hesitation, all disorder." Kroll is clear that objectivists and even centrists such as Le Corbusier (or Vanbrugh or Bernini) are distinguished not by their type of design (starkly simple or richly ornate) or by whether it contains "reference to tradition," but by their desire to control the whole project. Nowadays they may use "vernacular" references and add gargoyles or half-timbering or fountains to create a whole Disney World, but they are not permeable to what Kroll calls "the mysterious, the indefinite, the complex." I quoted earlier his astute remark that "we should be suspicious of nostalgic admiration for beautifully organized spaces conceived at a time that has nothing in common with our era," and he adds, "particularly when expressed by those who reject the vulgarities of the present...we *must not confuse eclecticism with ecumenism:* the one borrows, the other exchanges...it is all a question of power, of not confusing colonialism with ecologies.... Every time a new power wished to legitimate itself it fed its propaganda machine with these esoterica." The "exchanges" of true spiritual ecumenism are those switches of imagination in which we thought we were on one stage and found ourselves on another, and in that transition experienced the power to become—if we have the courage—actors in a different drama.

Kroll, of course, is talking about structures in the strictly architectural sense; he is talking about attitudes to creating spaces in which people live and work. And the reaction to such ideas has often been a panicky conviction that to allow all that "permeability" to people, places, history, would lead to chaos. "The mysterious, the indefinite," are not concepts we easily associate with building anything—houses or social structures or educational processes. But the fact is that Kroll, and others like him, have created building complexes that are entirely practical and yet open to change, to difference, permeable to feelings and hopes that require expression. In apparent paradox, Kroll often uses industrially fabricated components to do this—the subject of the particular book from which these quotations come is the possibility of doing just that. Kroll's approach is "populist," and he finds it possible to allow the expressed needs, aspirations and *differences* of prospective occupants (whether the buildings are to be homes or workplaces or colleges) to influence and inspire the form taken by the building. He talks of the "military attitude" in which "planners divided up the infinite diversity of human activities, assigning them to a series of precisely defined zones" and sent out stewards "responsible for indigenous affairs"..."who would listen in a patronizing and benevolent way to the wishes of the natives and set everything in order." Priests and ministers of all kinds generally perceive themselves as stewards "responsible for indigenous spiritual affairs" and most religious people expect that. On the other hand "the new order depends on new practices, new relationships: it cannot be imposed as a rational procedure. It has to be allowed to arise out of the smallest and humblest initiatives that grow together to form a mosaic."

In the mosaic, where are our spaces of the spirit? We can only discover this as we create the mosaic *together* "out of the smallest and humblest initiatives," expressed in stumbling phrases, inarticulate pleas and fears and hopes, and through memories and traditions handed down in families and neighborhoods, their origins perhaps lost.

This word "together" is crucial, and marks an insight that leads directly to consideration of how human structures can be hospitable, because hospitality, as we shall see, can and does emerge only from the working together of "the smallest and humblest initiatives" and those who are gifted to respond to them and help them to create a new whole. As we shall see, hospitality is never "centralist" or "objective." It has to be "permeable." This is a difficult and delicate undertaking, developing its own language to express the interaction, the insights. Perhaps we can learn to be more skillful as common tasks proceed, understanding better how the validation of significant action in one space can empower entrance into another, which becomes a new stage for a new cast. In the transition, imagination is transformed, caught suddenly in the gale of the spirit that blows fresh blossoms through the vaults of tradition.

There are no neat answers, because this kind of "permeability" means discovering how to reimagine together over time, allowing for "the mysterious, the indefinite, the complex." But permeability also means being very aware of what has worked, and why. We may redefine and reimagine and then rebuild the rooms of our lives but we have to do it together, in such a way that the insights of tradition may be heard and tested and if necessary revalidated. (An astonishing prophet of this project is Charles, Prince of Wales!) We have to have the drastic humility to let go of our pre-conceptions and our pet spiritual snobberies, to allow the play of (to quote Kroll again) "collective spontaneity, of streets, markets, populism, bad taste, unself-consciousness...mixture, ambiguity." Particularly ambiguity.

But we do have choices to make. "Permeability" does not mean allowing every fad and fear to impose itself. As Guil says, in the moment before he disappears, "There must have been a moment at the beginning, when we could have said—no. But somehow we missed it."

Our culture has missed too many moments, has not said "no" to the "centralist" colonizers or the "greedy objectivist" planners. There are many stages in our theater of ambiguity; the "kind of integrity" that revalues entrances and exits comes from making choices, and those choices are the ones discovered, not by tossing a coin (that can lead to dissolution), but by being in touch with the power in the thresholds of human encounter that are entrances and exits as we choose to perceive them.

7

A Criterion for Structural Choices

A t this point there is a need to gather up the insights explored in the previous chapters and to see whether, drawing on them, the notion of hospitality can provide a way of thinking about the human habitation in its various guises, the changes it requires, and the continuity without which it ceases to be imaginable.

The human habitation is in a dangerous condition. It is inhabited, if sometimes barely habitable, and part of the reason for the dangerous condition of human structures is the failure of hospitality.

The historical reasons need to be considered, and can be traced, the obvious villains being renaissance individualism and the rise of capitalism, strengthened by the enormous increase in the possibilities of private and corporate wealth that resulted from the exploitation of fossil fuels and mineral ores. The industrial revolution was an economic revolution because, with the availability of quantities of coal and iron, and later oil and other non-agricultural products, Adam Smith's notion that prosperity in terms of higher wages and profit was self-limiting (since there was an absolute limit to how much could be produced when crops, timber and water were the original and only ultimate material basis for all production) was falsified.

The limits now being reached two hundred years later are imposed not so much by the exhaustion of resources as by the disastrous effects of their uncontrolled exploitation, which is a very different matter. At the time of the industrial revolution there was a giddy sense that production (and therefore wealth) made possible by mineral and fossil fuels had no ceiling; this finally put an end to the last vestiges of that sense of a community obliged to care for its weaker members that resulted from knowing that in a resource-limited economy anyone might, in turn, become one of the weak ones. Wealth had already long insulated the landed aristocracy from any sense of inter-dependence with other human beings who did not own the land, but the new wealth of the "self-made man" (and many more of them) carried with it even less of that awareness of vulnerability. The philosophy of economic "laissez faire," and the enlightenment classification of the laboring classes as virtually another race, eliminated finally the notion of any kind of universal obligation toward one's fellow man, let alone woman. But it substituted the vast umbrella of "charity."

In considering hospitality as the key to healthy human structure and the criterion that shapes decisions related to the energy field of "home," the issue of "charity" is important and needs to be considered first, because it has been traditionally and powerfully the response to the human failure of existing structures. Hospitality itself has indeed often been a form of charity, from medieval monastic hospitality onward. But hospitality as a concept and a philosophy of life not only goes much further but if properly understood challenges the political basis of "charity" as a response to need, because "charity" assumes that structures need no change but only modification while hospitality proposes an entirely different political and moral structure for human living.

In discussing *charity* here, I use the word not in the old religious sense of a virtue but, for obvious reasons, in the usual modern sense of voluntary, practical response to need or misfortune. *Charity* in this sense is what most people recognize as an obvious way to respond to the poverty they see around them. *Charity* is a way to respond to social inequality, a way to repair spaces in the structure that leak and crumble. "Charity" has been important in all unequal societies, and that means most major ones. *Charity* means actions and structures designed to benefit the disadvantaged. Strictly, these are not part of the structure of the official economy, and not legislated, though legislation—such as tax deductions for charitable purposes—can help it, but the same motives that support these can support legislation to serve the same purpose.

Charity leaves room for individual compassion and initiative. In the western capitalistic system it is still regarded as an important or even preferred way to respond to the existence of poverty. This is true even when many governments have felt obliged by public opinion to provide programs of relief out of public funds—minimal or generous according to the current political climate. This is, in a way, a kind of charity since its motives are often similar and the pressure to create it has similar moral roots.

At different periods and in different ways, tax-funded "welfare" systems have responded to a sufficiently widespread moral awareness of an obligation to care for the victims of poverty through state-funded and organized structures. Various forms of public welfare legislation, pushed ahead by the vociferous moral appeal of, for instance, early socialism and egalitarian philosophies or the post-1948 awareness of a moral obligation to create a society that could live up to the rhetoric of the war as a defense of civilization, was made possible in practice by newly created wealth. But the economy changed, the enthusiasm that could accept high taxation for this purpose waned, and the capitalist doctrine did not support it. To call on citizens to ensure their own future fitted a return to an individualistic philosophy that viewed wealth as a personal possession to be earned and exploited for personal motives. The residual public welfare provisions were to be supplemented by charitable organizations large and small.

In the nineteenth century, before "welfare" legislation became acceptable, charity was the only safety network of those who became poor through the workings of the new industrial economy. The links between charities and state systems are clear, but so are the differences.

In many places working people created their own "welfare systems" through local organizations funded by the contributions of their members. Friendly societies, burial clubs, housing societies and various other cooperative systems created their own modest insurance against destitution. But they depended on the existence of enough regularly employed people to fund those who fell into poverty, and they could not help those who had not the means to contribute at all. Charitable organizations could and did step into the gap.

Charity may arise from the same motives and philosophies as tax-funded welfare, but it is different because the recipients of charitable help are not "entitled" to it, even in a theoretical sense, but depend on the decisions of the charity organization's officials or of charitable individuals. This is true even though officials administering state systems often behave as if recipients had no entitlement but were seeking charity. It is also different in that charities are not accountable to an electorate and can, if they choose, act in ways that defy the current moral philosophy.

In the aftermath of the industrial revolution "charity" became very powerful. "Charity" was effective. As well as appeasing the consciences of the wealthy it created schools and hospitals for the poor and scholarships for those considered capable of moving upward from the ignorant classes to something approaching gentility. It built homes and created jobs, distributed food and clothing and "tracts."

The word *tracts* is no longer familiar, but it is significant for understanding *charity*. In the nineteenth century language of charity it meant short pamphlets of exhortation to religious faith and virtue, usually with warnings of the consequences of sin, very simply expressed for the moral improvement of the poor. "Tracts" were distributed at revival meetings, or house to house, and often included in food baskets, and they were important in motivating material charity, because they helped the charitable to avoid the stigma of caring for the bodies of the poor while neglecting their eternal salvation.

"Charity" became a huge industry and, with its other secular persona, "philanthropy," and its offspring, "volunteerism," it involved and involves the expenditure of vast sums of money and all the bureaucracy that goes with that. Charity or philanthropy became a necessary thing for a wealthy and respectable person to be involved in. The new rich, then and now, felt it essential to endow colleges and libraries and to set up trusts and foundations in order to dispense millions of dollars or pounds or francs (or whatever other currency) to worthy causes. Much of this vast work was and is extremely efficient, carefully and intelligently administered, and does a great many useful and beneficial things; that remains true even though it has been beset by the scandals and muddles that are incidental to the handling of power and money in a society founded on the principle of self-interest.

That "charity" in these forms did, and does, fail to prevent poverty, homelessness, malnutrition, let alone the injustice and oppression that lead to these things, is obvious. If we are considering the state of the human home, its dilapidation, its leaking and crumbling roofs and walls, "charity" (or its contemporary successors) cannot provide the needed reimagining of the dwelling. It cannot do this, no matter how lofty the ideals of benefactors and volunteers, for the very simple reason that the money on which charity depends comes from those who have wealth, and those who have corporate or private wealth depend (however much they would like it otherwise) for its acquisition and the continuance of the existing economic and social structures. This is not in any way to question the motives or the personal integrity and even the vision of those who use their wealth or their personal time and energy, often in near-heroic ways, to alleviate the suffering they perceive. It is simply a fact. If the economic and social structures that underpin the existence of current forms of wealth were changed in such a way as to remove the causes of, say, urban poverty, that wealth would not only diminish (how, and how much, would depend on the kind and speed of change) but at the same time structures of philanthropy would no longer be needed.

Charity or philanthropy or state programs perceive the dangerous state of the human habitation and respond by repairing and strengthening as much of the structures as they have, or think they can spare, the means to do. Out of many possible ones, I take a few examples of structures of living that are perceived to be in disrepair and for which charity offers a response; in considering this I am including tax-funded programs based on charitable initiatives and arising from similar moral response by the voting public.

"The family" is a structure commonly perceived to be in crumbling condition. If the structure of the family is the issue, the problems are perceived in terms of the breakdown of traditional marriage, or as the rise in the number of teenage parents, or as unwanted pregnancies, or as absent fathers, or even as domestic violence. The response is to set up marriage guidance counseling, birth control clinics, homes for unwed mothers, abortion facilities (or alternatives to abortion according to conviction), parenting courses, refuges for abused women. The response is also to spend money to bring pressure to bear on legislators to fund these things out of taxes, and to urge other legislation such as laws to make divorce more difficult (or easier) to introduce stiffer penalties for abusive men, to provide less (or more) support for single parent families, to introduce sex education in schools (or ban it). All this may be useful, or essential, or deplorable depending on one's point of view, but none of it allows room for asking what a family is, or what kind of social structures might support familial relationships of a sustainable kind. These questions are beyond the scope of charities as they are of state programs.

If the structures in question are educational, nobody has any doubt that education is in a state of extreme dilapidation. The problems are perceived in various ways: students leaving school illiterate, violence in schools, low levels of general knowledge, not enough attention to "basics," not enough attention to the arts (or too much), too little discipline (or too much), too few young people trained for skilled jobs, too many leaving school at sixteen, teachers paid too little, private schools siphoning off the talent (or too few private schools) and so on and so on.

The response from charitable foundations and benefactors and some state bodies has been equally various: to fund scholarships at all levels; to set up "adventure camps" and other trainings that emphasize initiative, endurance, and team spirit; to create "alternative" schools and extra-curricular courses in art, music, dance; lobbying for funds for inner city schools, for more vocational schools, for more special needs classes, for tenure for teachers (or no tenure for teachers), for more student grants and loans.

Good as results may be in some specific cases (again, depending on one's point of view), none of this leaves room to ask fundamental questions about the nature of education, about whether schooling equals education, about the possibilities of entirely different ways of inducting the younger generation into the duties of adult life and the necessities of gaining a livelihood. Radical reimagining is ruled out; the only possibility is the renovation of existing spaces in the structure to make them more habitable.

Religious structures are very various in their symptoms of dilapidation. Church problems present themselves in such ways as diminishing church membership, clerical misconduct, redundant church buildings, doctrinal disputes, lack of "vocations" to ministry, lack of lay leadership, disaffection of women members. Not all churches display these—some evangelical churches are growing both in numbers and revenue; their problems are more likely to be perceived from the outside, and expressed in terms of a theology out of touch with reality but providing a sense of belonging and security that others may perceive as delusive.

In the case of religious structures the connection between the "charity" approach and the preservation of the status quo ante is less obvious because the money/project connection is less immediate. But churches, as much as any other institutions, depend on revenues from church members, from property and from their own and other charitable foundations in order to pay their bills and fund their projects. When the projects are unpopular the funds dry up. Especially in the major denominations the money and the conservative nature of the structures go hand in hand. For instance, funds will be found from private or corporate giving to build schools and to rebuild well-filled—and therefore prosperous—churches, while closing those with low attendance or inadequate "giving." Remedies for perceived ills are sought by such things as funding "renewal" programs designed to get people back to church, holding very expensive conferences to improve liturgy or religious education, making religious authorities more accountable for their actions (both moral and financial), and also by funding missions at home and abroad that provide for basic human needs as well as trying to be centers of spiritual renewal. All of these and other projects are generously funded by church-based foundations and other donors. Some are more imaginative than others—for instance the Campaign for Human Development, though created by the Roman Catholic Bishops' Conference of the U.S.A., funds neighborhood and community development projects, regardless of religious affiliation.

But church-funded structural remedies do not address fundamental questions of the role and nature of religion in this (or any) culture. All they can do or want to do is to repair the existing religious structures and make them more attractive and liveable, though some also reach out to people in need because that is part of the gospel mandate. The success of those churches that succeed in attracting members and money demonstrate (better even than the lack of support for others) that what is most easily attractive is the sense of being spiritually and morally secure and acceptable in a predictable world, and this can include the satisfaction of knowing one's church is helping people in need. But this security can only endure as long as fundamental questions are excluded. That is, no radical reimagining of the structure is permissible, even by the most community-minded churches or parishes, though individuals may entertain (and even express) doubts.

As these examples suggest, charity, under its many guises, (and including or allied with tax-funded initiatives similarly motivated) can have great power for good but not for change. It can repair but not challenge, rehabilitate but not redesign, because for its existence it depends on the continued strength of the social and economic forces whose effects it seeks to mitigate. Therefore if charity is not the way we can regain and re-create our home, if it insulates us from envisioning radical solutions because it depends for its existence on the structures it lives in, then we need a wider and more liberating concept, and hospitality, as a kind of metaphysical umbrella, does provide this.

Hospitality in this sense is a word and a concept to describe the energy that creates what I have referred to as a "field," whose nature has to do with the physical/emotional/ spiritual "home" in which humans are truly able to live. It is the criterion by which we can make choices that respond to the energy of that field and shape our home—a home envisioned through magic casements, founded in the depths of the past and of the psyche, permeable to the spirit.

Hospitality as a practical criterion is about how to share spaces and resources in ways that are just, sustainable and humanly satisfying, and that allows the outbreak of the essential anachronism of the sacramental thresholds without which utopia, even if achieved, is a well-run holiday camp rather than a true human habitation.

Hospitality has a very ancient history. Abraham, visited by three strangers, got up and ordered the killing of his best calf and much baking and cooking, not because he was particularly generous (he wasn't) but because the deep-rooted customs of desert people required that those who possessed food and shelter should share it with those who were at least temporarily without them. The reasoning behind it was clear: the one now at home and well fed might at any time become the hungry stranger in need of hospitality in his turn. Therefore, from the richest to the poorest, it was unthinkable that one should not share the best available with the one who came to the door. When, in another example from Hebrew scripture, the traveling prophet Elijah came to the house of a poor widow, he and she both took it for granted that she would feed him, even though what she had to share was the last food between her and starvation.

For centuries, even in many more settled situations, the sacred duty of hospitality was enjoined, and in warlike times and places it included the understanding that to share food meant to share peace: to kill or injure a guest with whom one had "broken bread" was a crime unspeakable. In the folk history of the highlands of Scotland, for instance, the infamous deed of the Campbells was remembered against them for centuries (it is not forgotten yet) because having presented themselves in friendship to the clan MacDonald and having been offered hospitality and shared food they then rose up in the night and slaughtered their hosts. *see Dante!*

It is generally among the poor, and among poorer nations, that the strongest tradition of hospitality endures. People who have worked in Nicaragua helping to build homes, roads and schools are among the many whose experience of the very poor is one of an open hospitality that will share whatever meager provisions are available. This matter-of-fact and ungrudging and usually genial hospitality astounded men and women from a culture that has learned to distrust the stranger at the door (not without good reason) and has extended the saying that "charity begins at home" with the tacit addendum "and need not go much further."

But the sense that hospitality matters endures—if not at home, then at a soup kitchen or shelter; if not by direct service, then by a gift of money to support places where the poor, the sick and the stranger can be served. This last, too, is a kind of hospitality (although it is usually experienced in terms of "charity") and it is one that can genuinely express the same openness to the need of another, but in practice it may serve the recipient better than it serves the giver because they do not meet, and hospitality implies a meeting on the same turf, in the same spaces, physical or spiritual or both.

If hospitality is about making it possible for people to meet, to share food, to talk, to look at each other, then it is about the crossing of thresholds with all that that implies, the reimagining of boundaries, and if necessary the radical adaptation of spaces.

It used to be common for rural or small-town households in Britain to expect to provide a sandwich and a mug of tea to tramps and vagrants, and this was usually done at the back door, so that the stranger did not enter the house at all. But some households did invite the stranger into the kitchen, which would not be damaged by dirty boots and which did not offer much in the way of opportunity for theft. In some places such guests were known–they traveled regular routes and came back each year at the same time. Then there were the delivery men, the plumber or carpenter who would also be made welcome–but in the kitchen. In the United States a less stratified attitude to differences between people has extended the hospitable spaces, as long as safety is not in question.

These safety precautions, and the delineation of appropriate spaces, are an important indication of the level of trust in the private spaces and the level of security in the more public ones. These overlap. Private trust depends on a sense of security, and when security is violated trust perforce gives way to suspicion. The woman who has been attacked in her home because she opened the door to a stranger will not lightly do so again to anyone she doesn't know. The housewives who hand the tramp his sandwich on the doorstep (or may refuse to do even that) and the volunteers at the soup kitchen have good reason for the limitations they put on hospitality.

The fact is, hospitality can be dangerous. The old "laws" of hospitality existed in order to provide a code within which both host and guest could operate safely, and violation on either part carried the penalty of social ostracism as well as dire spiritual sanctions. Hospitality can never be just a matter of good will and generosity (that is, of "charity") that preserves the gap between giver and receiver; it implies and requires a pattern of living that makes the practice possible and safe, and that means a different basis for understanding it.

At this date in the world's history it is clear that the notion of hospitality has to be extended to include environmental concerns also. If the betrayed and battered earth is to continue to offer hospitality to human beings, then those guests of a fragile ecosystem must, in their turn, respect the home in which they have been invited to dwell. If the human race didn't exactly get an invitation card, the bounty extended to it was certainly read as such.

We need to be quite clear about the difference between hospitality and charity, including state welfare systems created out of the same moral philosophy. The cultural transition from hospitality as social insurance for a community aware of a common danger of want to charity as a substitute for hospitality (and a way to assuage residual guilt) is complex and certainly cannot be traced here in detail. It would be a mistake to idealize the hospitality of the poor, even though poorer societies have been better at hospitality; the poor can be every bit as suspicious and protective of space and property as the rich. The important difference is that whether we are talking about the sacred customs of tribal cultures, or the frontier reciprocity of people living on the outer edge of survival, or the religious (medieval Catholic, Islamic, Judaic, Buddhist) equation of generosity to the poor with good chances of salvation and the acquisition of spiritual merit, in these contexts hospitality in some form is regarded as a duty or moral requirement.

The nature and extent of religiously motivated hospitality was often laid down quite precisely. Tithing, of crops or of money income, by the medieval church, for instance (resisted and disliked as it often was by peasants who had little), could sometimes be misappropriated to subsidize clerical lifestyles, but the original intention was that tithes should support not only the local church but church institutions for the poor—hospices for strangers, schools, lying-in hospitals for poor women, aid for the local indigent—thus providing *community* hospitality. The aging rich knew very clearly that such hospitable actions are an essential part of the soul's ascent toward salvation.

Some of this rules out the deeper impulse of compassion, ˌ the generous response to the suffering of another. The point is that the laws of hospitality—which by extension include giving beyond the boundaries of the home itself—are first of all built into social and religious expectation, quite independently of the feelings of the giver or the worthiness of the recipient. Charity, however, at least in the debased sense given to that word by nineteenth century class-conscious giving, is not a basic requirement, it is not a law, it is not taken for granted. It is a laudable moral choice, a virtue very creditable to the giver. It is an *extra,* which may be spiritually very desirable but whose lack is not culturally alienating to those who refuse it. The person who refuses to offer charity may be hard-headed like Scrooge, but he is not socially outcast except by choice.

And the character of the recipient becomes important. The "undeserving poor," to which category Alfred Doolittle proudly claimed to belong, have been succeeded by "immigrants who sleep ten to a room" and "welfare freeloaders" of America and Britain who, it is believed, either "render themselves homeless" (such fun sleeping on a heating grate) or have babies in order to have an income and a home; their behavior thus justifies the refusal to vote funds for social programs.

The concept of hospitality is about basic human expectations, not primarily about personal generosity or about just deserts. Yet it codifies the human desire to cross boundaries, to meet, to experience compassion and act on it. The codification is important because it does not negate the generosity, but removes from it the sense that the human acceptance, the sacrifice, the *giving* are one-sided and greatly to the moral credit of the giver. There is no special moral credit in doing what a common humanity requires and the human soul naturally craves. Children can never at first understand grown-up limits on hospitality. They have to be taught about separations, however necessary. An Indian father once described how hard he found it to explain to his small son why it was not necessary or right to give money to other children lying hungry and sick in the streets, but eventually he succeeded in convincing the child that these people were different, that his own happier situation was God's will and not to be questioned. The father felt it necessary to do this in order to protect the child from the torment of unavailing compassion in a situation that, as the father saw it, could not be changed.

This is why hospitality provides a criterion for helping us to judge the validity of our imagination when we make decisions about whether and how to rebuild our habitations. For hospitality is a measure of the human ability to create spaces for the nurturing of many kinds of relationships, including relationships with plants and animals, rocks and oceans. It is about breaking down unnecessary walls, but it is also about *preserving* walls and boundaries because hospitality means that an individual or species is invested with the space occupied and developed by another. Hospitality is about doors, and where they are placed, and who has the right to open them. There are therefore roles and responsibilities on the part of host and guest, and they are different. The doors are opened, the thresholds are crossed, but they must not be eliminated, or hospitality becomes impossible. The benefit to both host and guest depends on the awareness of the meaning of those thresholds: the meaning, as hosts, of inviting across them, or, as guests, of crossing them. So the questions that need to be asked about a reimagined structure for living can be focused by thinking about hospitality. Who is the host here? Who are appropriate guests? How do we decide on who and how? How is it possible for the transition to be safe for both? Can the status of guest change to become that of householder and host?

Roles are not always clear. Who is the host on the farm—the farmer or the crops? Who invites and accepts whom? In a family, who is host? Are children guests—or hosts? How does guest become host? In a school, who are the hosts—the students or the teachers? Or are they both guests of Wisdom, waiting on her invitation and inspiration to enter new spaces? In a city, can all citizens be hosts when so many are not able to decide their own comings and goings, being more like tramps at the door than householders? And are wealthy businesses in a city acting as guests—or as conquerors, even when the city government "invites" them? Do they come in through opened doors or smash the walls and rebuild them to exclude the former "hosts"?

Importantly, hospitality in some way bestows on the guest the dignity that enables him or her to be host in turn. That is part of its function: hospitality is about relationship, not primarily about permission to occupy a space or receive a service. So the switching of status happens here as in the exits and entrances of a stage. The relationship of hospitality can switch from host to guest, though the space seems to be the same one.

If every exit is an entrance somewhere else, then the boundaries of hospitality can open into unexpected places. At Abraham's desert dinner party he waited on his guests, giving to the three strangers all the honor due from a prosperous man with many servants and cattle, but it was the strangers who became the benefactors, giving to Abraham and barren Sarah the child for which they had long ceased to hope. The reversal of roles is enshrined for Christians in the words of Jesus, child of a culture and a law founded in the custom of hospitality. He was well aware of the tendency to despise those to whom alms are given, and aware too of the contrast to this in the way people vied with each other to entertain him and do him honor. With irony, he pointed where the real honor lay: "Whatever you did for the least of these, you did it for me."

How do you know, he was warning, who bestows honor and who receives it? Who is generous and who is gifted? The roles are different—but they can switch unexpectedly.

The paradox of hospitality is the interface of security and danger. To make the spaces of life hospitable is to put them at risk, yet not to do so is to doom them to spiraling suspicion amounting to paranoia, retreat into ever tighter spaces from which finally all contact with reality is excluded, for there are no doors and no windows. Then, because there is no awareness of the reality of the building, which has become a paranoid delusion, it crumbles and falls.

A sense of belonging, of being at home, is required for hospitality, because "my" home is by definition the locus of hospitality, but that space is perhaps also common space, as I shall be discussing. The hospitality is a shared one. So the guest may choose, and be chosen, to share that common space and responsibility.

A church declares its identity through creeds and rituals; it includes and therefore excludes. But it can offer hospitality in a very literal sense to those who do not share that identity, and some did so in the Sanctuary movement by which churches in the U.S.A. illegally chose to shelter, regardless of creed, those fleeing death squads in El Salvador. Some churches offer hospitality regularly by developing feeding programs and shelters on their premises or, in another sense, by providing intellectual and spiritual space for dialogue with those of other or no faith.

Can there be a switching of roles here too? Is the guest the bearer of blessing? Is the space made sacred by the act of hospitality, not the other way around? The requirement of hospitality as sacred is handed down, it is the tradition, but the tradition must be validated by each new action. Time is disengaged by anachronism, turned backward in illogic. But the anachronism heals the sick tradition, and time is recovered as sacred.

This kind of thinking may easily seem interesting but not of practical consequence, yet ultimately any real change in the way we imagine and rebuild the structures of our lives will depend on our ability to keep on pursuing such speculations with honesty.

To keep our feet literally on the ground it is helpful at this point to look at some ways in which people are already reimagining and then practicing aspects of everyday living in ways that are structured by hospitality, in the sense I have begun to develop here. None of these examples and ideas explicitly state the criterion of hospitality, yet it is clear what is going on. These are "magic casements" in a functional sense, even when what's seen through them is a verifiable fact.

One such magic casement opens as the result of a new and small movement of decentralization of what has come to be called "de-urbanization." The very nature of such a movement implies a different attitude to ownership, for the obvious practical reason that in most cases such ventures are not lavishly funded and therefore depend for survival on the assumption of a common responsibility, and this in turn breaks down old conceptions of ownership and opens the way to hospitality. As this movement has been explored in books and articles and in some real experiments, the tendency may be to expand existing small centers of population rather than create entirely new ones. Public facilities and agencies (schools, clinics or hospitals, police and local government) have to be remade to meet new demands. It is recognized that people will have to pay for this in both money and time, and that therefore the more time they are willing to put in the less they will need to pay in local taxes. The more part-time volunteers, firefighters, police, medical aides, teachers, teachers' aides, etc., are available, the lower local taxes can be. To achieve this vision people have to organize together, work together and be accountable to the community for running the institutions they need, and for raising the money to pay the indispensable professionals and maintain the plant. In this way public areas come to be thought of and politically structured as common. They are experienced as extensions of home, places and functions that belong to the community and express the sense of belonging that "home" implies, because old concepts of ownership have had to be superseded. New people come in as guests, but become responsible as hosts.

This tends to create a situation in which public accountability is easier to ensure, very simply because people know each other. If some are apathetic and withdrawn from common life, greedy and clever people can always profit, but the remedy is in the hands of those who have let themselves be unaware of what was at risk. This is *home,* and those who live in it are together responsible for it.

Such a de-urbanized community, like other communities, must depend on land for its food, but in a more localized economy the farmers and market gardeners are bound to be responsive to local need. They can have no captive markets, as agribusiness does. Already, some farmers have created what is called "community related agriculture," in which local people pay the farmer to grow crops, and then receive the food produced as it is ready. It is like buying shares in the farm, and getting the interest in the form of food. This enables new farmers with little capital to buy or rent land and buy machines, seed, and other needs. The need for up-front money is sometimes met through monthly income from shareholders, with the local bank putting up the capital on this security. It sounds crazy to conventional thinking, but it is being done and it works. People who buy into such schemes sometimes choose to pay for part of the food by giving labor instead of cash, especially at peak times of the farming year. In this way the farmer need not employ labor he or she does not need all year round. This kind of scheme implies a fairly small scale, but, if it is done skillfully, a small scale repeated many times produces a great deal more food more economically than large scale farming. Here, there is a hospitality that gives the "guests" (the customers and occasional laborers) the dignity of responsibility, yet they depend on the farmer or market gardener for the invitation to take part. Yet in another sense the customers are inviting the farmer to share their resources, which he needs. No charity here but a radically reimagined structure based on mutual hospitality, and as in all hospitality there are boundaries, there are decisions, to open doors that might have been kept closed.   *In Canada they are dying because Walmart, etc.*

An interesting example of this shift in imagination is the growth of food cooperative groups in modern Japan, some of them quite large. Some are deliberately designed to break down the barriers between the producer of food and the consumer. In these, consumer members are encouraged to go to the farm where the food is produced and to get to know the farmers and how they work and live. They can also be involved in organizing the distribution of the food. Farmers get to know the people they feed and to understand their needs, and consumers learn to appreciate the farmer's work, as well as feeling that even as town dwellers they are in touch with nature. Their mutual respect and cooperation means that it becomes possible for consumers to accept that food production is affected by the season, the weather and climate change; they learn not to expect a uniformity and consistency that can only be obtained by treating the fields like a factory, as agribusiness does. Increasingly, not being able to count on factory-type consistency is a price people are willing to pay for safe and wholesome food. In Japan some cooperatives offer classes on cultivation and processing to all members, so that there is a real shared understanding and a sense of common goals that go beyond any normal market mechanism. Again, there is the element of hospitality. People are invited to enter a new area of living.

One of the societies, "The Society for Reflecting on the Throwaway Age," makes a clear connection between the way people treat the earth and the way they treat each other. When the fruits of the earth are treated with disrespect as merely commodities, so also are people—they become things to use and discard. This group has developed the experience of reciprocal hospitality to ensure that the interests of producer and consumer are seen as one. Some consumers are involved in the actual farm work and even accounting and one interesting detail is that products are delivered in bulk, with the dirt on, to neighborhoods, so that residents must organize the distribution among themselves with the specific intention that doing this together will enable them to talk about the food and its preparation for the table; this helps to create community among the consumers. Summer camps to involve children in the farm work and teach them about agriculture are also part of the co-op.

There remains a big gap between such close-knit, effective but isolated organizations and the possibility of creating a strong feeling among the general public that, beyond the concern for healthy food and good producer-consumer relationships, issues of meaning in work and life are actually important public issues. But this is implicit in the attempt to understand and foster a flow of energy from private to communal to public and back, opening doors by hospitable decisions that enhance the "home" quality of life.

The Japanese experiments and others mentioned above are certainly not the only way to manage the practical relationships among people and food, land and dwellings, private and common, and all have their drawbacks. In a bad year, for instance, the farmer in a community-based farm may not be able to satisfy his or her "share holders." Provision for this, and skillful management of alternatives, are essential. But the principle on which such developments are built is important, and no matter how things are planned a healthy community, in every sense, needs the sense of home, which means that everyone belongs and that the system (whatever its shape) belongs to them since they are responsible for it and, once accepted as part of it, they are the "hosts" to others who may need their example or their services.

To help imagination I want to take two examples—one real and common (in more senses than one) and one fictional—of the use of certain limited spaces that matter a lot to the people concerned, but that are not privately owned by them and not within houses, in the sense of buildings with walls that enclose domestic space.

One example is the village green, which still exists in many European villages and some American ones; the other is "the secret garden" in the book of that name by Frances Hodgson Burnett, still read and loved after a hundred years and now also a film.

The village green provides a good place to perceive the meaning of hospitality and question its implications. It is pre-eminently a common area. For many generations—and still in some places and to some extent—it was the place where village householders could pasture ducks and geese and even larger creatures. The common well was sometimes there, and there was often a pond where animals could be watered and children could skate or slide in the winter. It was usually the place for public punishment—the village stocks were there. But the green was and remained primarily a meeting place. Public announcements were made there, local recruits drilled there, itinerant preachers could gather an audience there, traveling showmen, basketmakers, tinkers and sellers of patent medicines could ply their grade and politicians could make speeches there. The village pub (or pubs, according to population) was or were usually built on the edge of the green, very conveniently for political candidates who wanted to provide liquid reward to their supporters, and it was and often is the place to celebrate political and military victories. Large villages could even host a yearly fair, though regular markets were and are almost always held in towns. It was, and still is, also a place for less formal gatherings, a place to stop and exchange news, sit on a bench of a summer evening, exercise dogs, sail toy boats on the pond.

All of these things can be and were and are done elsewhere, some of them indoors in buildings made for the purpose or in private homes. But when they happen on a village green they become something between the "private" and the "public" as normally considered, because the green is not for just anyone. Even in situations where use of the green is not restricted by law and custom, the people who live around it have a strong proprietary interest in it. Attempts to encroach on it—to make a road across it, put up a tourist information center, cut down trees—arouse strong and energetically organized opposition. This may fail if the village has grown large or even has been swallowed up by an encroaching city or town, and people around the green lose out to the desire to attract revenue, or simply to town-bred bureaucrats who see only a useless stretch of grass, but the feeling is real. This is "our" green, it belongs "by rights" to the people who walk on it, sit on it, play on it, gossip on it and especially *look* at it: that is the feeling. Where the green is spoiled or reduced the people who live near it feel as if a part of their home had been destroyed, and that is, in fact, what has happened. Whatever the law may say, and whatever the legitimate concerns of other people in the area, the people who live around the green know that it "belongs" to them, and they belong to the community that it symbolizes and visually expresses. The feelings about it are strong shapers of lives, of political choices and of the values that also shape the attitudes of households, including children. A village green is a strong educational influence.

So this is a clearly defined area of land that is not privately owned but is part of the experience of "home" and shapes the human sense of what "home" requires. Yet however strong the feeling of "ownership" and "home" may be, nobody wants the green to be divided up between owners of the houses around it. It is precisely its common character that gives it value. (Something similar operates when Masai people in Kenya resist government attempts to deprive them of their common lands by dividing them up and giving ownership to individual tribes and people in order to make them more amenable to exploitation.) If it were not a place where all kinds of people might meet, it would lose its value, but equally, most of these people whom one may meet are *known* people; they, also, "belong." Not all of them need be friends or even friendly but they all belong, either because they live there or are friends or relatives of those who do, and enjoy coming there.

That "belonging" involves acceptance of both written and unwritten restrictions on behavior. Nobody, for instance, may dig up the green except maybe by common consent in time of emergency, to grow food or provide shelter from bombs.

Nobody, in other words, may treat the green in ways others would dislike, and few would want to, because it is the fact of common consent on the use of it that makes it possible for "everyone" (meaning "us") to enjoy its amenities. The restrictions may even extend to what people do to their "own" homes—the colors they paint their doors, and how many cars may be parked in a street that edges the green. It is all quite complex and yet basically simple. This is "our" green and we love it and will take care of it and woe betide the invader! But we are happy to share it with friends, and even tourists, within limits; this is our local hospitality.

The boundary between private and public has melted here. Certainly there is still a distinction between the area of the family home and the area of what is common, but the energy generated by the sense of belonging, of ownership, flows out of the door and down the path and onto the green. It is part of the "field" that shapes people and dogs and even doors to become what they need to be for the "home" experience to happen. There are smaller and larger examples of such common spaces: there are lawns and gardens that run along the back of a terrace or row of homes, the care and use of which may be shared by the tenants in each apartment or each house; there are the hundreds of acres of Ashdown Forest in Sussex in England, where centuries of struggle by the "commoners" against barons and kings and bureaucrats and developers have managed to preserve a beautiful stretch of woodland and heath for common enjoyment (including the enjoyment of visitors, birds and squirrels) and for the pasturing of animals.

Through such experiences the "common" meaning of home has stretched and grown, yet it still includes the sense of security, of identity. But it is also fragile. If too many tourists come, if too many shops are opened, if too many cars come through, the expanded sense of home is lost. Too much noise, too many soda cans and paper bags, less and less grass, and above all too many unfamiliar, indifferent faces, and soon the sense of ownership is lost. People retreat behind higher garden fences or their front doors; when they need relaxation they don't sit or play on the green but get in their cars and join the tourists looking for wilderness; if they want company they go to the homes of friends, or play bingo, or go to the cinema or the theater or dance hall or rock concert. To be "at home" requires familiarity, identity, security, a measure of control over one's surroundings; when these are lacking there is fear, suspicion, chauvinism and the creation of defenses. Only when people feel "at home" can they risk being hospitable; without secure identity and a sense of control, hospitality is a surrender to hostile forces, and no one is the better for it.

An extreme and horrific example of this was the collapse of any "neighborliness" in former Yugoslavia, where, under communism, an imposed national identity plus strong centralized (not local) control made it possible for ethnic memories and hatreds to remain suppressed and invisible but unresolved, so that when exterior control was removed it was all too easy for demagogues to break fragile and newer bonds between ethnic groups by appeals to old unrevenged crimes. The sense of being hospitable, of welcome for people of varied origins, was quickly disrupted in the name of an exclusive "ownership," intended to recover lost security but quite unable to do so in practice. All that is left is fear and the desire for further revenge.

The deep importance of secure at-homeness as a means to growth and thence to hospitality is the theme of *The Secret Garden*. This children's classic has been reprinted over and over again for successive generations of children, because the adults who buy it for their children recognize in it a fundamental truth about what is required for safe growing up—*both* safe *and* growing.

The central character is Mary, both spoiled and neglected by Anglo-Indian parents who consigned her to the care of Indian servants and took little interest in her. When they both die in a cholera epidemic Mary is shipped home to her only remaining relative, an uncle who has become a recluse since the death of his young wife in childbirth. He lives in a big rambling old house on the wild Yorkshire moors, and this is where Mary is installed in the care only of the starchy housekeeper and a young servant, Martha Sowerby, child of a moorland family.

Angry, rejected, lonely, and without experience either of

warm human relationships, of any degree of material want or of how to care for herself, Mary cannot deal with Yorkshire Martha's rough kindness, or with the need to put on her own clothes, or to occupy herself all day. Driven out of doors by boredom, there are meetings—with an old gardener, Ben Weatherstaff, as cross and rude as herself but sturdily independent, with a robin and with the wind and fresh air off the moor. Martha buys her a skipping rope out of her own small earnings and gradually Mary's health, damaged by the Indian climate and by neglect, improves. She also discovers a carefully kept secret of the house when, one night, she hears and traces the hysterical screams of her sickly cousin Colin, the son who survived his mother's death but whom his grieving father has refused to see. Also unloved, though kept in luxury, Colin has nursed a conviction that he will die young and, indulged in all his whims, has become a semi-invalid tyrant who refuses to go out-of-doors and lives in a darkened room. The two spoiled, lonely children are well matched, and when Mary finds and confronts Colin she is not intimidated by his tantrums: having yelled at each other they form a tentative alliance in their isolation.

The real change for Mary begins when, in early spring, following her friend the robin down a long walk behind walled gardens, she finds a door hidden by ivy, and near it the glint of a half-buried key. She has heard stories of a locked garden, but the gardener would tell her no more. Alone, unaccustomed ever to ask permission for what she wants, she manages to turn the key in the rusty lock (this story abounds in striking symbolism) and enters the secret garden. It is still winter, and all seems dead to her, but it is her secret place where, once inside, no one can disturb her, for no one knows she is there. But below the bare winter trees the first stirring of spring is happening, and Mary finds little green points appearing here and there among the dead leaves and grass. Knowing only Indian lush growth she feels an excitement at these live green shoots and begins to clear little spaces round them "to let them breathe." Meanwhile, driven by guilt and a helpless and reluctant anxiety about the child to whom he has given a home, her uncle sends for Mary to ask her if she has all she needs, and

Mary, greatly daring, asks him for "a bit of earth" to dig in and plant. She will not tell him of the secret garden, but wants to legitimize her find, and he agrees, thinking she will make a space for herself among the many flower beds. Mary asks Martha about how things grow—she has some pocket money and Martha agrees to buy her some small tools with it.

Soon afterward, Mary meets Martha's brother, Dickon, who has come to bring the tools and some packets of seeds. Moorland-bred, Dickon is a lover and "tamer" of all wild things, including Mary, and he creates in her a trust that decides her to invite him into her secret kingdom. Already her hurt, hungry little heart is learning to trust, and that trust makes her hospitable. To her, Dickon's coming into "her" garden is not a threat but a sharing, an enhancement of her delight in her garden rather than a dilution of it. And Dickon, skilled and wise, respects her "nest" as he respects the nests of the birds he knows and loves. He shows her that the dead trees are not dead but sleeping; there is green wood inside the gray bark. He tells her the meaning of the little green shoots, and together they work to clear and tidy and prune and plant, with the robin for an approving audience, for the robin whose territory this also is knows these humans will not harm it—it too can be hospitable.

The rest of the story is of the unfolding of young lives as the leaves unfold and the blossoms come and the roses follow. As Mary's healing progresses, so does her hospitality. When Mary feels she can trust him, Colin is let in on the secret, and the children delight in evading Colin's nurses and servants when he demands (to the amazement of all) to be taken out in his invalid carriage. He allows only Dickon to push it and forbids anyone to follow them. In the secret garden Colin watches the coming of spring, which he claims is "magic," and in the strength of that magic he chooses to stand on his own feet. With amazement Mary and Dickon watch the invalid stand, then walk, and week by week gain strength while pretending still to be an invalid when he returns to the house.

There is much more—and it all matters, because this is one of the great stories. In the end, one day, Colin, now fully recovered and running a race with Mary, bursts out of the garden door and meets his father, who has been drawn back home from his restless travels by a mysterious request for his presence from Dickon's mother, who has meanwhile become the children's ally and friend. And so these alienated children are drawn back into life by the garden.

But it was a secret garden. It was because it was a secret, their own place, that the healing and the growing were possible. Until the end of the story no grownups are allowed in except Dickon's mother, who is to the children not a grown-up but more of an earth goddess, their protector, their secret-keeper. (She is also a provider of picnics when keeping the secret of Colin's improved health makes it imperative that he should not display a healthy appetite on returning to the house!) And there is Ben Weatherstaff, the gardener, for this was the garden that with his help Colin's mother once loved and planted, and in which a rotted tree branch caused the accident that led to her death. But Ben is not, any more than Mrs. Sowerby, part of the "real" adult world. He is part of the garden, as Dickon is part of the moor: crusty, earthy, faithful as the seasons.

This sacred place of healing and transforming has to be secret, apart, uncontaminated by the anxieties and expectations of the adult world. And this secret quality is fragile; in the story the children's deception shows that they instinctively know this. One day, as the ending implies, the secret must be told, others must be allowed in, but not until the work is done, not until the prisoners of loneliness and neglect have been set free by their common discovery of the earth that is their heritage.

This could not have happened inside a house; symbolically these children needed for their healing more than could be supplied by adult caring, even if caring had been available. In our time these children might be sent to therapists for help, and no doubt that might work, but the point of this story is that for human beings to grow up healthy they need to learn the meaning of their humanity in places where being "at home" and "belonging" is protected from the false assumptions and expectations of "normal" society. And to grow as human is to know oneself as part of the growing earth.

These are two very different examples of the significance of a space that is home, which is common in a sense specified by the function it performs, and which is not privately owned in a legal sense by those who use it. Even to think of such places in legal terms is to be aware of the extraordinary lengths to which our society has gone to restrict and distort the reality of home. Both these examples exhibit the enormous importance of such an ambiguous space for human development, security and identity. But they also show how very fragile the reality is, when it is not protected by a wider social awareness of its importance for a healthy community. They demonstrate once more the reality that "home" is best described in terms of a "field" that shapes "things." It is not in itself a thing, yet it helps us to understand what David Jones meant when he said that the "thisness of an object is its own magic and connection...about how everything turns into something else." This is a threshold, a sacrament, a place where anachronism has a chance to break down barriers and allow the sacred, in very ordinary, even routine, ways.

Both these examples, the village green and the secret garden, help to challenge the validity of the public/private separations and make it possible to look at issues of family and land from the same perspective, as home, and capable of hospitality.

Land and the ownership of land and homes—there are no homes without land—have become defined in western society, and in other societies the west dominates culturally, by the need of business to organize people for maximum availability for employment—employment designed not to provide for the needs of the community but to secure maximum "productivity," regardless of the needs of the employed. For this purpose housing was placed where workers could be easily available to factory or office. And workers needed to be near their work. Incidentally, this made possible the kind of neighborhood and industrial organization I have mentioned, but that was not its purpose in the economy.

When higher earning workers would not tolerate the conditions of the industrial city (no recreational space, tightly packed homes, pollution) the suburbs came into being, providing more space—but all of it private space, unless people combined to create clubs, sports facilities, and other shared facilities. In the postwar world the women often became isolated in their new homes, lacking common spaces to meet or work.

Later, when mortgages cost more, women also took jobs beyond the neighborhood, and the great day-care jungle began, with women becoming the family taxi drivers and children dependent on schools and outside organizations for their experience of community. Everyone depended on cars to get to work, to leisure pursuits, to entertainment. In recent times, this personal mobility did allow women, employed or not, to meet, share experiences, and organize.

But "mobility of labor," that essential feature of modern "productivity," also drastically reduces the possibility or even expectation of community, of home beyond the house or apartment, families beyond parents and their children, of neighborhood identity or any sense of "belonging" intermediate between that of the household and that of something as large as nation or denomination. Local churches in the U.S.A. tried to fill the gap and to some extent succeeded, but only at the expense of any sense of geographic neighborhood community or commonality beyond denomination. Land and home have become imaginably separate, except for the little bit (and for the wealthy, the big bit) on which people build homes, and the even more removed experience of apartment or flat living. But land is still a basic reality, from which most people are excluded.

The recognition of the fluidity of the concept of home and belonging, as my two examples unfolded them, is essential in order to change the rigidity of our thinking about what is private and public, what is family, what is home, and what belonging means. Our thinking about home and use of the land, the "country," and therefore our use of it, depends on this also.

To start with family, having suggested earlier the inadequacy of the "charitable" approach for dealing with problems in the "family" area, we can begin by recognizing the importance for emotional and spiritual health of the sense of home, and also that it needs to flow out beyond the area of needed privacy into common areas, and we can also, on that basis, begin to reimagine the meaning of family in terms of hospitality. In a situation in which there is a sense of continuity, stability and common belonging such as that symbolized by a community around a village green, a family may safely be allowed to be something more than a system of biological relationships, important as those are. It can flow out into and mingle with other families and form lateral relationships that enhance and support the "internal" biological relationships. Children with few or no siblings can develop continuing relationships with other children who share the same kind of trust and continuity, secure friendships that help partners to renew their efforts to create and maintain stable households.

With the pressure off nuclear families to be the only upholders of stability and continuity and the only representatives of tradition and guardians of the nation's future (pressure sufficient to ensure speedy divorce in many cases) it becomes easier to accept the existence of "unconventional" households, those consisting of unmarried heterosexual partners, of homosexual partners, several families sharing a home, single parent households, or—something barely thinkable in the present sexual climate—adults who want to share a living situation but don't necessarily want to share sex. And in all of these households we can envisage children growing up. If "home" includes the common areas of life (both spatially and culturally) then we can look to the home in a new sense as indeed the basis of social stability and continuity, the place where people belong, the first (but not the only) source of a sense of identity and therefore of the possibility of hospitality.

We can also set about ensuring that there is a "secret garden" for the nurturing of young or damaged lives, a situation that is home, but defined by the needs of those who use it, and ensured by the community. We can think of this in terms of very literal gardens, areas of field and wilderness where children can experiment, build shelters, grow things, learn to share and to take responsibility together beyond the immediate view of anxious parents and teachers yet protected by common precautions and good will. In Marge Piercy's book *A Woman on the Edge of Time* she imagines a fantasy future in which children on the verge of adulthood are sent off to fend for themselves in the wilderness for a period of testing and of the assumption of personal responsibility apart from loved adults. But the children are, in fact, watched from afar so that help can reach them if they become seriously endangered. This is a kind of "secret garden" experience.

We can also think of the "secret garden" more symbolically as the area of living in which there is freedom to dream, and be different, yet not feel endangered or disapproved. But it is important to recognize that the symbolic and the literal are not really separable because people (especially children but adults too) need space where they don't feel supervised, where they can work out something different with the support but not the interference of the community or the family. Adventure playgrounds and adventure programs try to provide some of this, but, because they are in practice limited in space and scope and often involve risk, they have to be controlled and directed. What is also needed is the opportunity to discover new skills and new options for living, not constrained by the requirements of potential employers or the anxieties and ambitions of parents.

The implications of such "secret gardens" are that children might begin to conceive of adult life in very different ways, might even want to make those concepts actual, and might learn to cooperate and share projects and skills in such a way as to gain the power to make them so. This would entail an educational revolution, requiring from the wider community a flexibility of response that can only happen when that community itself is truly home, confident and trusting of its own identity to the point where it can allow itself to envisage change without fear. It means that the community has to feel empowered to take responsibility for its own economic future, based on a social analysis that has been able to demystify the established concepts of business and "productivity." This is a huge undertaking, and while some communities have in fact done some of this quite successfully, such an effort is so threatening to the power and profits of major corporations and the governments they control that on a large scale it can only be a long-term goal. Such a shift is fundamental to the thesis of this book, however.

The spiritual and physical structures we create will only provide a home for human beings when we allow the strong emotional signals to teach us what is required, and act on them, and perhaps at some point the "thousandth monkey" syndrome will come into play as the "field" of "home" reaches and changes more minds and hearts.

These signals are connected to the nature and practice of hospitality as an integrating strategy between public and private, between owning and sharing, between security and openness, one that offers hope of realistic criteria for the use of land so that it may be home for all people. And home, in that sense, means also the sacred spaces, the thresholds of transformation, the shifting vision of old and new, coming and going, chronos and anachronism.

8

"Come In"

*T*o carry forward the exploration of the meaning of hospitality as a criterion for structural choices, this chapter
chooses three ways for considering the ideals and realities of
hospitality as real experience.

These three ways of conceiving, planning and living hospitality as a definitive description of how to build the earthly
habitation are respectively fictional, historical and spiritual/
aesthetic in character. But, interestingly, all of them also share
all these descriptions, because the historical event must be
imaginatively re-created from memories and observation in
order to convey the spiritual power and seed imagination,
while the more spiritual/aesthetic draws on history for understanding and projects future possibility, and the fictional is
clearly and inevitably preserved as historical awareness. They
are all magic casements and they all test out thresholds where
anachronisms allow the sacred to be experienced.

The fictional creation of a society where hospitality is so
basic it need not be mentioned or even thought of is from the
fantasy novel *The Dispossessed* by Ursula Le Guin. She opens
her magic casement on a view of an anarchist society on a
planet called Anarres. It needs to be remembered, in reading
this, that "anarchist" has nothing to do with the usual popular
image of bombs or the chaos of unaccountability. It is a political theory about how people can live by their own free decisions yet in an orderly way and without dominating one
another—an idea most people find inconceivable. But in this
imaginary society all that is needed, including aesthetic and
emotional needs, is available through a personally accepted

social contract rather than by socialist regulation or individual enterprise.

Anarres is the twin "moon" of another planet, Urras, which closely resembles our Earth, at least in being fertile, beautiful, and, in the case of the particular nation that features in the story ("The Nation of Aieo"), capitalist, class-ridden, and deeply sexist in a way beyond what contemporary western society would admit to; yet the reader cannot but be aware that every apparently exaggerated sexist phrase from the culture of Aieo is heard daily in our contemporary "Terran" society.

The particularly significant perception that the magic casement reveals in the place called Anarres is the recognition, very hard for people reared to think of electoral democracy as axiomatically desirable, that to do without central government (even a "democratically" elected one) or police or law is not to do without structure. Connected with this is the awareness that structures of human life are not "natural"; all are taught and learned, all are in need of critique and correction, all are vulnerable to the forces of stupidity and fear. Le Guin's description of the origins of this ambiguous social experiment shows that it was created because the parent society on the "twin" planet needed a way to rid itself of determined revolutionaries, followers of Odo, the woman whose writing and example originally gave hope and vision to the group. Odo did not live to see the vision put into practice, but the existence of her followers threatened not so much the existence of the nation's actual political and social and religious structures as, more importantly, the basic assumption on which it was based, and which must not be questioned: the acceptance that "our" way is "natural"—that is, inevitable.

The place chosen to off-load these dangerous people was a moon, a planet habitable but, unlike the "parent" planet, stark and uninviting. For a long time serving as a source of minerals from its mines, but not officially settled, the planet was "empty." "There followed," Le Guin says, "the proposal...of giving the moon to the International Society of Odonians and buying them off with a world, before they fatally undermined the authority of law and national sovereignty on Urras.... For over...twenty years the twelve ships granted to the Odonian settlers went back and forth between the worlds, until the million souls who chose the new life had been brought across the dry abyss."

Odo's vision had called for radical decentralization but not de-urbanization. She suggested that the natural limit to the size of a community lay in its dependence on its own immediate region for essential food and power, but that communities be linked by networks of transportation, and that no community be "...cut off from change and interchange." However, the network was not to be run from the top down. There was to be no controlling center, no "capital," in the political sense, no establishment for self-perpetuating machines of bureaucracy and the dominance and drive of individuals seeking to become captains, bosses, chiefs of state.

But all this had to be developed not on a fertile and resource-rich planet but an arid and barely habitable one, where "...communities had to scatter widely in search of resources, and few of them could be self-supporting, no matter how they cut back their notions of what is needed for support." Yet, product of a high civilization as they were (and unlike many utopian visions), these people had no intention of regressing to a pre-urban culture without technology. They built roads to interchange products and ideas and arts so as to balance the scarcities of one area with the resources of another in "...that balance of diversity which is the characteristic of life, of natural and social ecology."

That can't be done without a center. So there was a centralized computer system to organize all this, and the place where it was located became the capital, in the cultural but not in the political sense. The essential point is that such a system of productive balance and technological sophistication can work as a human structure not because it is "natural" but because everyone teaches, and learns, that it is necessary to make choices in relation to the community's needs because only so can the individual survive. There is room in such a system for the eccentric who exercises his or her freedom to be different, but the pressure of public opinion pushes toward behavior that is at least not harmful to the social organism. Even the anti-social person who chooses not to contribute is allowed to make that choice unhindered, but at the cost of the satisfactions and even delights of common endeavor. There is always the danger—the book is hinged on this—that social accountability may become social coercion, regimentation in disguise by a public opinion that has lost sight of the vision of freely chosen commitment, but Le Guin's anarchic structure is one that has adapted (as our earth may well have to adapt) to comparative scarcity, yet without "controls," rationing, forced labor or hoarding of either goods of land by a minority of the powerful.

The whole story shows how the central character, the physicist Shevek, recognizes the way in which the social imperative to share could degenerate into a refusal to allow any individual thought or initiative, and so decides to travel to the twin planet, Urras, to the capital of one of its nations, Aieo. He has decided to share his breakthrough theories with physicists there. He realizes, in the end, that they only want his theories in order to dominate and control other nations and even other worlds, but meanwhile he gets in touch with the remaining Odonian underground in Aieo, of whose existence, like the carefully hidden poverty in the beautiful cities, the authorities had tried to keep him in ignorance. He escapes from the university where he is virtually a prisoner, though in privileged intellectual and physical luxury, and joins the Odonians in a huge popular demonstration that is brutally put down. Shevek only escapes with his life through the risky devotion of other Odonians and takes refuge in the "Terran" (Earth) embassy. There, talking to the ambassador, an Asian woman, he hears of a planet that, like Anarres, had to deal with scarcity, but for very different reasons.

What the ambassador describes to Shevek is the result of failure to build the "earthly" home on the basis of careful and respectful hospitality as a way of perceiving the planet's resources and using them before it is too late.

This is how she describes her home planet:

> My world, my Earth, is a vacuum. We multiplied and gobbled and fought until nothing was left, and then we died. We controlled neither appetite nor violence; we did not adapt. We

destroyed ourselves. But we destroyed the world first. There are no forests left on my Earth. The air is gray, the sky is gray, it is always hot. It is habitable, it is still habitable, but not as this world is. This is a living world, a harmony. Mine is a discord... people are tough! There are nearly a billion of us now. Once there were nine billion. You can see the old cities still everywhere. The houses and bricks go to dust but the little pieces of plastic never do—they never adapt either. We failed as a species, as a social species....Well, we have saved what could be saved and made a kind of life in the ruins, on Terra, in the only way it could be done: by total centralization. Total control over the use of every acre of land, every scrap of metal, every ounce of fuel. Total rationing, birth control, euthanasia, universal conscription into the labor forces. The absolute regimentation of each life towards the goal of racial survival.

This book was written in 1983, when the possibility of global warming was only suggested and no one even guessed that ozone depletion would happen. In the event, Le Guin's bleak picture is probably not nearly as bleak as things might (may) become, in physical terms. But the important thing is the way the remaining humans in this scenario have dealt with the destruction of their world: by total and rigid centralization as the only means of survival for those that can survive. Le Guin's picture of a "Terra" degraded, the result of the failure to perceive interrelationships or transcend private and corporate greed as Anarres does, is a situation in which hospitality is no longer either a spiritual or material possibility. Responsibility for the means of survival has be surrendered to central authority because people have not trusted one another enough to make survival a mutual as well as a common gift.

To write about the bare outlines of such a rich and complex book and such an imaginative and subtle cultural structure is to distort it—the book needs to be read, and "needs" is the appropriate word in a society so lacking in vision as ours. It is not uniformly attractive to people like ourselves, whose ideas of beauty, comfort and satisfaction are formed by a planet as fertile and culturally rich as Le Guin's Urras—at least until this point in earth's history.

Le Guin describes the city of Abbenay on Anarres with its

"...wide, clean streets. They were shadowless, for Abbenay lay less than thirty degrees north of the equator, and all the buildings were low...pretty much alike, plain, soundly built...almost all of one story only because of the frequency of earthquakes. For the same reason windows were small...but there were a lot of them, for there was no artificial lighting provided from an hour before sunrise to an hour after sunset. No heat was furnished when the outside temperature went above fifty-five degrees Fahrenheit. It was not that Abbenay was short of power, not with her wind turbines and the earth temperature-differential generators used for heating; but the principle of organic economy was too essential to the functioning of the society not to affect ethics and aesthetics profoundly. 'Excess is excrement,' Odo wrote in the *Analogy*. 'Excrement retained in the body is a poison.' Abbenay was poisonless: a bare city, bright, the colors light and hard, the air pure. It was quiet. You could see it all, laid out as plain as spilt salt."

A society without status or titles, without possessions, a society in which a child speaks of "the father," not "my father," and this may refer not to a biological parent but to a man who has related to the child in fatherly, caring ways. It is a society at first sight sexually promiscuous because people are not to be possessed sexually or otherwise, yet a society in which the moral imperative of *promise* is essential and so allows committed monogamy even with all its pain and stresses. "Though it might seem that [Odo's] insistence on freedom to change would invalidate the idea of promise or vow, in fact the freedom made the promise meaningful. *A promise is a direction taken, a self-limitation of choice.* As Odo pointed out, *if no direction is taken, if one goes nowhere, no change will occur.* One's freedom to choose a change will be unused, exactly as if one were in jail, a jail of our own building, a maze in which no one way is better than any other. So Odo came to see *the promise, the pledge, the idea of fidelity, as essential* in the complexity of freedom." (My italics.)

The concept of hospitality as a criterion for choices in reimagined structures depends on the acceptance of the need for social accountability for decisions, and on the reality of promise. Le Guin's description of the development of such an inherently hospitable society in which no person is refused the means of subsistence (no matter how "bad" his or her behavior), and each is committed to making that subsistence possible, is closely linked to the comparative scarcity of resources; sharing becomes a means of survival as well as an ideological commitment. But this can only happen without coercion or sanctions if the possibility of free and permanent and adult choice is fully accepted and taught: so the educational structures that can instill the need for such choices (social, artistic or relational) have to operate by offering thoughtful and daily choices even to children. Hospitality is the built-in social insurance of pre-urban and culturally isolated cultures, but in a high-tech, closely interconnected and socially stressed world such as ours, which has inherited an ideology of finders-keepers and let the best man win, a simple realization that sharing is needed is not enough. It is so much easier to let the many die in order to maintain the inherited lifestyles of the few.

This is not "unnatural." As anthropological studies have shown, the idea that certain kinds of social structures are more "natural," than others is hard to sustain. In some circumstances a highly competitive, aggressive or (to our western way of thought) cruel attitude that pushes out the weak and eschews compassion is a means of survival in harsh conditions. It works. In others a non-violent way of life is a way of ensuring that everyone contributes to ensure the best use of scarce resources. It works. It is, however, possible to see that certain kinds of social behavior increase or decrease the possibility of human fulfillment—physical, moral and aesthetic. Hospitality as a social criterion allows not only for survival but for the development of artistic and relational patterns that enhance human satisfaction. Hospitality envisages as the basis of human structures a social contract involving (to anticipate the categories of Christopher Day to which I refer later) the straight, rational direction derived from the attention to what is needed for survival but also the curved, embracing line of spiritual awareness, the pledge or promise based on a vision of human possibility.

The magic casement opens on a land never inhabited—and never to be inhabited—by human beings, yet it allows an imaginative freedom that can then perceive the human world in a very different way. Le Guin's anarchist society creates structures for living that are hospitable in that they accept the restrictions necessary for common life yet build them to nurture the individual spirit. The architect Christopher Day in his book *Places of the Soul* asks why we often feel more comfortable in old buildings, why we may linger in the street of an old village yet rush along a new street toward whatever goal we had in mind, inattentive to buildings on the way. His answer has to do with the irregularity of older structures, the surfaces weathered, roof-lines and walls uneven and "out of true," frontages uncoordinated, planes meeting at odd angles. (The fashion for "distressing" perfectly good new walls and furniture to look as if time and use had worn them reflect this, at first sight, peculiar attraction.)

Christopher Day explains the reason for this:

> Imagine a small white room, almost square, one high level window only, no view—a monk's cell. Softly undulating plaster, a subtle curve on the ceiling and above the window; the ceramic tiled floor laid on not quite straight lines; the sunlight enlivened on the uneven surface of wall and floor.

> Imagine it again, the angles knife-edged, the wall shining smooth; ceilings, walls and floor meeting with each other in hard precise lines; the sunlight a sharp rectangle.

> The first is a room for prayer, a place of tranquillity set aside from the hubbub of the world. The second somewhere you cannot wait to get out of.

Why do we feel like this about irregular lines, surfaces and spaces? There is a tension between the need for stability and strength in building a structure and the need for "liveableness" that reflects the nature of human movement and body space. "We need the straight line and its rectangular forms. But these are not forms which we find anywhere in the human body, in human movement, in human activity, nor anywhere in nature."

The attraction of old buildings, the revulsion many feel from what they perceive as "modern" architecture, is not due to nostalgia (though nostalgia is, after all, an important emotional indication that something is felt to have been lost) but to the spiritual discomfort created by a system that consciously rejects what cannot be reduced to mechanistic elements, with the implied ability to plan and control all of life. The usual science fiction fantasies of "cities of the future," and indeed the built fantasies of skyscrapers of steel and glass and sharp, clear angles, make strong statements about the priorities of those who conceive an ideal future in such a way; it states at every glance that what matters is only what can be measured and planned for straight-line purposes—no curves. Such building dwarfs the human scale and is intended to do so. Putting trees in the foyer of a vast bank or allowing office workers to keep plants on desks in cubicles without windows does not change the intent, it merely indicates that nature (human nature) can safely be allowed a little indulgence since its real enslavement is so total. The fact that more recent corporate architecture has attempted to mitigate this mechanistic symbolism by introducing color and quasi-oriental or baroque detail with domes and arches and traceries and gilding only serves to demonstrate that the intent to control and dominate is sufficiently self-aware to make it necessary to employ a little subterfuge. Factories have learned to use color and better qualities of light because these have been shown to improve productivity. If better productivity happens because these things also make people feel happier and more relaxed, that is secondary. The controlling motive is as rectangular as ever. In contrast, the functionally rectangular buildings of Le Guin's anarchist city (but I would guess that the plaster was fairly rough and the hand-made doors not perfect) house workshops where all kinds of beautiful things are made, ornamental as well as useful. Indeed, in Anarres, beauty is seen as functional for the human spirit, not just to keep the workers working.

The straight line and the curve need not be antithetical; in fact they need each other if the structure is to be not only solid but spiritually liberating and growth-nurturing. "The balance between organizing principles and fluid life-forms itself needs to be not just one quality measured against another, but at every moment a weaving into a single whole." Day says that "a patchwork of dead and amorphous pieces, like alternate functionalist and organic buildings along a street, or a jungle indoor garden in a geometrically severe atrium, is no conversation."

> I cannot draw a living curve on a computer, though the computer can copy it later. The line I draw can bring together the straight and the curve, as my arm itself does. The swing of my hand on the paper can create a straightness that is strong but not mechanical and angles can be a meeting of "conversing" lines that bend as the arm bends—curves and straight lines not just added to each other but rather the straight (firmness and organization) in the curved and the curved (life enhancement) in the straight.

A human hand can draw such a line, human hands can build structures composed of such lines, and they will stand and they will live.

There is one specific aspect of this kind of building that can help to illuminate the creation of non-physical human structures—remembering always that, as we have seen, the physical spaces and the analogous spiritual ones are not, in fact, separable.

Promise, the deliberate commitment to the choice of a certain direction, is the measure and exercise of freedom. Promises build a structure within which lives can be lived with purpose, but they are future-directed, they are about movement in one direction rather than another; therefore they imply the construction of ways to go. This is the reason why real choice may not in fact exist in certain kinds of structures. It may be necessary to open magic casements in order to be able to envisage possible choices, and then to design and build or rebuild the direction in which those choices lead us. As Christopher Day says, "A narrow, not quite straight, invitingly textured and lit corridor for unhurried uses...can be a real delight; a smoothly surfaced, evenly lit, straight corridor for large numbers of people in a hurry is quite the opposite, and makes even the most well-meaning building into an institution."

The way chosen, the way built, expresses not only the goal, the place to which it leads, but the process of getting there, the way in which that passage is experienced. Is it only a means, a passage to an end? Or is it a valuable experience in itself, one to be relished, and one which will influence the way in which the goal—the place at the end—is itself conceived and designed? The building of the way in which one chosen direction takes us may well modify the goal, for "as the building progresses we can actually experience entry and movement sequences, the ways views are focused, sunlight penetration at particular times of day and year...we have the opportunity to emphasize and moderate these experiences."

What Christopher Day is describing are ways in which a structure becomes hospitable, not just in intention but in the way the experience of getting there shapes how things are designed and made.

As illustration, this notion can be explored in terms of a particular kind of human structure, a theological/ecclesial one.

In 1993 the Church of England, working with the divisive issue of the ordination of women, came up with a compromise, which allowed the ordination of women but also allowed those parishes or individuals who did not agree to opt out by choosing to refuse the ministry of a woman. (It was more complex than this, but for my purpose that will do.) Nobody was very happy with this arrangement, and people on both sides complained that this way in which the authority of the church was exercised lacked clarity, failing to give the sure guidance that it was called upon to provide. Those opposed to women's orders felt that the resulting confusion, organizationally and in terms of what the church's governing body theologically could or could not decide, was even worse than allowing women's ordination. Roman Catholics, even those sympathetic to women's ordination, also felt that "the church" had an obligation to come to a clear decision and that this particular Anglican compromise merely left the real issues dangling and weakened the ecclesial unit.

How does this look from the point of view of creating a hospitable structure in which people can feel welcome but in which the hosts are responsible for wise decisions for all? If we think about the building of a way toward that goal, it is possible that the experience of *choosing to go that way* is just as important as how the space will look when we get there, and in fact the process of going there will modify that space. The complaint that this decision by the Convocation undermined the authority of the church is made from a mindset that perceives a way forward as a straight, well lit corridor leading to a place to which one progresses at the fastest possible pace.

It is possible to envisage the theological authority of a church in another way, to see it in terms of the building of a corridor in accordance with the direction chosen, according to a promise made in full fidelity. But the building of a way toward that hospitable space in which an organic unity of faith and practice is possible is itself part of the experience necessary to design and build that space, which will in turn lead to other spaces. The building of this way must itself be a hospitable experience. It will be difficult and confusing, the materials may be scarce or arrive late, the skills needed must be learned. To be hospitable to many kinds of people this passage must allow for views in different direction, for light from many angles, for entrances and exits at intervals. It must be human shaped, with bends, with different levels of floor and ceiling. (The "high" and "low" churches can make their own contributions, not averaged out but idiosyncratic and irregular.) It can allow for pauses, with deep window seats and even little rooms in which to relax on the way. The experience of building the way is a learning and a creation of common languages and common history.

What shape will the space called church have when the end of this passage is reached? We won't know until the skills and insights learned in constructing the passage can help us design the place we enter. But meanwhile we have magic casements. Churches, like other institutions concerned primarily with their own survival and built on a centralized and hierarchical model, find it hard to conceive of authority except on that model, or of unity except in response to that model. It requires the magic casements of mystics and prophets to perceive the vision of a more humanly shaped structure, one that is built from sensitive response to reality—the reality of the experience both of God and of human need.

It is very difficult to let go the apparent (but delusive) security of clear central authority, uttered in edicts and definitions accepted by all. The delusion lies in a failure to perceive that, historically, theology has in fact always been the expression, caught like a photo at a given moment, of an ever-changing movement of thinking and feeling and experiment. The unevenness, the twists and turns, the alternations of dimness and light, are how it unfolds. When a place of belief is occupied it is already changing; people are making another door and working out how to adapt the known space in relation to another that is needed, or that has been excavated from a mound of almost forgotten habitation and found to be needed, after all.

So the criteria with which to test the soundness of the building are not those of unchangingness or conformity of style, but those of hospitality made real by promise. Those who are the hosts, the ones inheriting the tradition, bear the responsibility of building and rebuilding a structure that is faithful to the gospel command of inclusiveness interpreted through the ambiguity of a loved yet flawed tradition.

In the terms of Ursula Le Guin's physicist, Shevek, "unless the past and the future were made part of the present by memory and intention, there was, in human terms, no road, nowhere to go...." Tradition and change turning on the axis of promise.

A supreme example of this is my third window that opens on a real life story about tradition and change turning on the axis of hospitality. Yet what we see through this magic casement is not mere fact, like the floor boards we stand on as we look out, but a tale of terror, courage and transformation that is true myth just because it is made of historical facts and real people, and illustrated with photographs and documents. It is a myth about hospitality, archetypal in its simplicity and power.

This is a story that shows how hospitality is the way in which the village green and the secret garden may survive as spiritual places and not wither into tourist attractions or private clubs. This is the myth that is the stuff of the walls and roof of the human habitation, because hospitality is not random but the free and faithful acceptance of both risks and possibilities. It happened, once upon a time, in the village of Le Chambon Sur Lignon in the Haute Loire region of France, during the years of German occupation—1940 to 1944.

[handwritten margin note: Le Chambon]

In 1940 the German forces had taken over what became known as the "occupied zone" of France, but for a while left a so-called "Free Zone," which was under French control as long as the French authorities did as the German ones required. This was easier and cheaper for the Germans than having to police the area themselves. The French authorities in charge appealed to patriotism to "regenerate" a disciplined and purified nation, loyal to its leader and free of the presence of Jews who had, it was taught, been responsible for the weakening and corruption of pre-war France.

Le Chambon was in the "Free Zone." It is a village at the center of a peasant community that also attracts tourists in the summertime. It is a windy, bleak place in winter, and life is hard, even at best.

It was, very unusually in France, an almost entirely Protestant village, and this Protestantism was the Huguenot kind, very aware of a long history of resistance to authority in the name of conscience, of the persecution that resulted and of the solidarity that enabled people to maintain that resistance, and to survive.

All over France, in those years of war, networks developed to hide Jewish people (both French Jews and those fleeing Germany), furnish them with false papers, and if possible help them to reach Switzerland or Spain. There were Catholic convents and monasteries, schools and other institutions and many individual homes whose heroic work saved many lives and cost the lives of not a few who did this work, but these centers and networks of rescue, though often known to one another, were otherwise isolated in a population that was at best silently supportive of such work but unwilling to be involved (being silent was risky enough) and at worst hostile and liable to report suspicious goings-on to the authorities. The difference between what was done by these heroic people and what happened at Le Chambon was that the coherence of the Protestant community, which comprised most of the village, made its rescue work an open secret. Everyone knew what was going on though not all were actively involved. Some disapproved of the fact that Jewish families—especially Jewish children—were living there, yet the presence of the Jews was not concealed. In fact when a representative from the Vichy government came to demand the rounding up ("rafle") of all Jews in the community, he was presented with a letter from some older students of the Cevenol School, a local boarding school founded by the Church, stating quite simply that they would not obey:

> We feel obliged to tell you that there are among us a certain number of Jews. But we make no distinction between Jews and non-Jews. It is contrary to the Gospel teaching. If our comrades, whose only fault is to be born in another religion, received the order to let themselves be deported, or even examined, they would disobey the order received and we would try to hide them as best we could.

Over the years, hundreds of children and adults were hidden, sometimes passed on to teams who would get them out of the country, but sometimes staying throughout the years of occupation, especially in the case of the children. Households who received the children did their best to create a normal life for them, though at times an anonymous warning of a "rafle" would come and the Jewish guests would be quickly evacuated to outlying farms or even into the forests until the trouble was over.

Gradually a system was built up. Refugees were passed on by the secret networks across the country; they arrived by train or on foot and were taken into homes temporarily, supplied with essential false names, "papers," ration books and clothing, and then distributed to other homes, where further plans could be made. There were some losses. Some Jews were found and deported. Later, when the German regime occupied the "Free Zone" as well, a few of the organizers were arrested and some killed. But the "success rate" was extraordinary.

Le Chambon provided hospitality for people in desperate need, shared its own minimal physical and plentiful spiritual resources with those whose race and culture and often language were different, but also it maintained and strengthened its own sense of identity and belonging. For four years, through alarms and terrors and through the everyday hardship and ingenuities of survival under wartime shortages, and including all the inevitable friction and conflict, Le Chambon was a community of hospitality. Its conscious model was the biblical "cities of refuge," places commanded (in the books of Numbers and Deuteronomy) to be set aside for the protection of those who had unwittingly caused a death. Scripture required that such places be established "lest innocent blood be shed," and if that applied to those who committed accidental homicide, how much more did it apply to those who had done no harm at all? Thus this biblically-minded community argued, and it was no coincidence that the thirteen people who became the *responsables* for organizing the hiding and care of incoming refugees were those whom the pastor, André Trocmé, had long been gathering fortnightly to discuss a passage of scripture together. These in turn gathered others in their own part of the parish, for sharing, study and interpretation. These groups grew in size and energy, and the non-violent theory and effective practice by which the whole community operated its refugee work emanated from them.

All this did not happen without leadership, and the pastor, André Trocmé, and his wife Magda in their very different ways represented the core of that leadership. André's long and painful road to a commitment to non-violence and to the provision of refuge was the result of deep faith and the willingness to act on it no matter what the consequences. His leadership was uncompromising, exercised both through powerful preaching and through personal example. (He always refused to deny what he was doing and was in fact at one point arrested and sent to a detention camp with his fellow pastor, Edouard Théis. Both were later released by orders from "somewhere higher up" but no one knew whose or why.) However, André's leadership was aimed at empowering others to make their own reflection and personal decisions. It was a shared ministry of compassion in which the praying and planning and risk-taking were also shared. It was, in effect, an "anarchist" type of leadership, one based on the freedom of promise.

Magda Trocmé, on the other hand, was a practical woman to whom religion was more of an ethical than a mystical support. It was she who, in a sense, launched the whole extraordinary enterprise without intending to but as a simple result of her ethical stance. In the second winter of the war a German Jewish woman knocked at the door of the presbytery. This was at a time when Jewish people who had fled from the Hitler regime in Germany in the late thirties had already made their way to remote places in southern France, including Le Chambon. But in Le Chambon, as well as a temporary welcome in homes, a few had stayed to become students or teachers at the Cevenol School which Trocmé and others had founded.

So Le Chambon was, by 1940, already a name that was mentioned to people fleeing persecution.

Here is Magda's description of the experience that made Le Chambon into a "city of refuge" on a night of snow and bitter wind:

"A German woman knocked at my door. It was in the evening and she said she was a German Jew, coming from northern France, that she was in danger, and that she had heard that in Le Chambon somebody would help her. Could she come into my home? There was lots of snow. She had a little pair of shoes, nothing....I said, 'Come in, come in, of course—naturellement, entrez, mais entrez.'"

It was the normal response of the hospitable. But it was a first step that began a long journey. When the frightened mayor of the village indignantly refused Magda's request to help with obtaining indispensable "papers" and told her to get the woman out by the next day, Magda knew where she stood—in the tradition of biblical hospitality.

She returned to the presbytery to find that the "little pair of shoes," put to dry in the oven, had burnt up, an accident less funny than it might seem, given the acute shortage of shoes in wartime: buying them was illegal for adults and the black market ones were too expensive. Thus began a search through the village to find shoes, papers, and a place willing to accept the dangerous guest. All these were found, but this hurried and unorganized rescue made it clear that something better was needed.

So the planning began, creating a system of safe places, of guides, of false papers, and though forging false papers went against the Huguenot community's deep-rooted objection to lying, it was to save lives, and that mattered more to these people. From that time hundreds of Jewish people came to the presbytery and were accepted into the network of hospitality that the village had become.

The major actors in providing homes were, not surprisingly, women. One of them, asked later why she was willing to take in the refugees with all the danger, the watchfulness, the lying that was entailed, answered simply, "Who else would have taken care of them if we didn't? They needed our help and they needed it *then.*"

To this woman and to the dozens of other households involved, this hospitality was simply something that had to be done. "What else could we do?" The surprised question, in various forms, was their reply to the later incredulous inquiries.

All this careful and efficient organization of hospitality was, in effect, a continued act of resistance to the Vichy government and to the Germans who stood behind it, because the inhuman nature of the authorities' policies canceled, for the Le Chambon Huguenots, any duty of civic obedience. The primary motive, however, was not resistance but hospitality.

There was another form of resistance going on, for in the mountains and forests, and infiltrating the towns and villages, were the Maquis, members of the armed resistance who fought against the occupying forces and their servants with every weapon they could find and were openly committed to violent means when necessary. They also helped to hide and guide Jewish refugees, but that was part of their campaign to overthrow the enemy. The Maquisard occupied, in effect, a very familiar type of human structure, based on the need to overcome or be overcome—defensive, heavily guarded, and only hospitable as a means to another end. The Chambonnais, on the other hand, were building a structure specifically designed for hospitality; they constructed doors to open, knocked down walls when necessary, created new spaces and new ways to get to them. But there was a meeting of the two kinds of resistance on the ground the Chambonnais had created. Non-violent themselves, they chose to shelter and protect the Maquisards when that was necessary and in turn called on Maquis help to lead their Jewish guests to safety. As another expression of hospitality, even in death, André Trocmé took the risk of going to conduct the funeral of a parishioner who had turned Maquisard and been killed in ambush, but he found that the local Catholic priest, not knowing or caring whether the dead man had been Catholic or Protestant, had already conducted a funeral. That sort of encounter of risk-takers crossed normal barriers.

The experience of Le Chambon demonstrates the function of hospitality as the interface between perceiving the future as the creation of viable structures of resistance and the future as organizing to change unjust and destructive structures directly.

The Chambonnais were a local, mainly self-sufficient community of moderate size. They, like all limited and homogeneous populations, ran the risk I referred to in connection with "village green" models, of becoming chauvinist and narrow. The spiritual challenges of the refugees, focused by the community's faith, helped the Chambonnais to discover a sense of identity as a people committed to a mission of hospitality, one that stretched their notion of "belonging" far beyond the lines of local culture and parochial loyalties. Their sense of history and their sense of religion brought into their lives an awareness of membership in something greater, something overriding. Yet it all came down to a very local network of trust, and it relied on the continuity of a way of life in which people needed that trust and that neighborliness for survival in a harsh climate and difficult times. But if that trust and continuity grew to encompass the stark needs of "outsiders" it was because both were rooted in spiritual principles as well as the skills of communal survival. Here again is the contrast between Le Guin's Odonians on bleak Anarres, and the "Terran" response to comparable conditions. The difference is a spiritual one, and it doesn't come "naturally" even though it corresponds to deep human need. It must be taught and studied, constantly chosen, evaluated and chosen again.

The Chambonnais passage toward the future is the "Odonian" one; it is a direction chosen, and shaped on its way by events and insights and irregularities (of place and spirit) that could be understood in the light of a consistent but flexible spirituality and incorporated into the work as it progressed.

Hospitality requires an ability to perceive and respond to demands beyond obvious self-interest, and that means there has to be a taken-for-granted set of principles supporting the idea, which then becomes part of the continuity. Le Chambon had that in its religious commitment, focused by the symbol of the biblical "city of refuge."

Hospitality, therefore, offers that further dimension *within* the everyday operations that can break open the effective but limited social structures of a familiar community and let in the strange, the suspicious, the ambiguous. Like the suddenly soaring cathedral facade encountered round the corner from the bicycle shop, hospitality suddenly confronts a coherent and well-known community with the challenge of the necessary–unnecessary, the awesome, the peculiar. It lets in, with the strangeness of beauty and compassion, the strangeness of evil, and by so doing shows up evil that is so familiar it has ceased to seem evil. When the second German Jewish refugee came to the presbytery, Magda Trocmé went to the wife of a well-known French rabbi who was staying in Le Chambon, after having escaped from the Occupied Zone. Could not this Jewish connection help other Jews? Magda asked. The woman angrily refused—these refugees were *German* Jews! she said. "It is because of the *foreign* Jews that our French Jews are persecuted. They are responsible for our worries and difficulties!" So evil slips in, and needs to be recognized, and that means caring for the ethical structures that make hospitality real and not sentimental or facile.

Hospitality demands the creation of appropriate structure, as happened in Le Chambon and as I suggested in the last chapter. Guests must be cared for in appropriate ways, and that has a cost (in space, food, energy, personal risk, time), and the social and spiritual value attached by the community to the practice of hospitality has to make that cost, which may be very heavy, seem worthwhile, so that a failure to practice hospitality comes to seem like a betrayal of the common identity, a sin so egregious as to deserve social ostracism.

Hospitality will often demand the creation of new structures. A hospital, a spare room, a larger kitchen or a common kitchen? New kinds of worship, new ways of making decisions, new kinds of education? These structures are themselves the means to educate the citizens and convey a strong message to the "incomer."

Hospitality can be, as it was in Le Chambon and on fictional Anarres, a focus of communal identity that insists on working out cultural and spiritual values and then celebrating them in practical and ritual terms. The practice is in itself a strong instrument of resistance to a corrupt and self-seeking usage of power, and shows up the pseudo-public and the pseudo-spiritual for the pretense they are. The existence of communities committed to hospitality in this sense is a constant challenge—and threat—to the power structures that try to sell themselves as committed to the public good—humane, "democratic," enlightened.

Hospitality is worked out in a social bond created by individual promise: that is the very difficult choice that can allow the radical and very practical reimagining of inherited spaces, spaces that are both endangered and rendered inappropriate by changed times and by the new insights forced on us by those changes.

It is a spiritual and moral choice. It is not "natural" in the sense that the word is used in the phrase "natural laws," or in the sense that there are no workable alternatives. There are plenty, but this one *is* "natural" in the other sense that it is a choice deliberately and consciously made on the basis of the known interdependence of all human beings with one another and with all creation, which are indeed "natural" facts. The choice and the promise can only be made, and kept, by means of a constant dialectic of learning and teaching, listening and speaking, intuition and reason, the straight and the curved in conversation.

As the discussion in this book has shown, the metaphorical and symbolic senses of structure, space, building, threshold and other terms are linked to the literal ones in ways that constantly transcend the merely metaphorical. If we are looking for the concept and practice of hospitality to illumine our choices and guide our promises we need to be deeply aware of this. As we saw that the position of a room in a house could indicate the value attached to the work done in it and to those who did the work, so it becomes apparent that in practice the way we build houses (and churches and schools and offices and places of government) expresses our prejudices, our priorities, our aspirations. Changing the way we think about each other and other living beings and about the earth changes the way we build, and the buildings change the users—and so on.

Hospitality as a criterion pushes us to judge the structures we have inherited, to recognize the cause and nature of their dilapidation. It will change both the way we build our homes— public, private or communal, indoors or out—and the way we live in those homes. Inversely, as we judge old attitudes and perceive the genesis of the evils that cause our house to crumble, hospitality as a criterion for moral choices forces changes in attitude, the making of new promises, and so changes the shapes and relationships of the spaces in which we choose to live. We adapt, or build anew, but the choices are made on the new, old, dangerous and realistic basis of hospitality.

9

The End, the Beginning

*T*he changes required of human culture if it should adopt hospitality as a criterion for judging the worth of structures are enormous, yet they are quite ordinary. They involve choices that have been made by many human beings and human societies as far back as we have any record, and these choices are still being made.

In our time, however, hospitality is normally perceived as a morally laudable option for individuals, and the reason for this narrowing of view has to do with the acceptance of a mechanistic interpretation of the universe, allied to the notion of man as the highest and controlling factor, for which everything else exists. With this goes the hierarchical model that narrows the control to fewer and fewer and more and more powerful people who make decisions to use the earth not only exclusively for human benefit but for the benefit of the most powerful humans at the expense of other humans. To these the world is a machine that we can—more or less—understand and ultimately (they hope) control, and if there is not necessarily an Almighty Artificer who made it and keeps it ticking, then there are plenty of willing surrogates. The choices made in the past and still being made at this moment by these Divine Surrogates have brought the earth to the brink of destruction.

Bill McKibben, at the close of an almost despairing book called *The End of Nature,* in which he feels that humans have already so much altered "nature" that it can no longer be called by that name, dares to reimagine the dominant-dominated relationship between humans (he calls them "man," not without reason) and other beings. He hates not only the reckless refusal to control pollution and degradation of the planet but

185

also the plans to "manage" the planet sustainably, for "men's" use with genetically engineered trees and crops and manufactured clouds, once it has been perceived that conservation and profit go hand in hand. His own decision is to keep the broken promise of global hospitality by reducing as far as is possible his own impact on nature, using less, traveling less, yet trying to love what is left that can still be called "nature." Nevertheless something in him will not be satisfied with this stoic spirituality. Opening his own magic casements he can see a time when "the ten thousand years of our encroaching, defiant civilization...could give way to ten thousand years of humble civilization when we choose to pay more for the benefits of nature, when we rebuild the sense of wonder and sanctity that could protect the natural world."

To "rebuild the sense of wonder and sanctity" is to reimagine the spaces of our lives. It means to perceive the interrelation of people and places with an almost unimaginable freedom. It is ultimately a spiritual work. "Wonder and sanctity" are of the spirit; they describe the state of soul needed to explore degraded and misused structures with compassion and hope, to have the courage to open magic casements, to break down walls that separate, to dare to reimagine the meaning of thresholds, to experiment with new and old categories. Humility is needed also, since the lenses of ideological pre-conceptions can blind us to the new vistas, but we human beings not only may not but ultimately cannot impose on the earth the structures we have developed for the exclusive glorification and comfort of ourselves.

If we are, amazingly, somehow, able to free ourselves of pride and fear, we may discover that the imagining and creating of a hospitable space is delightful, arduous, dangerous and essential, on the small scale and on the large one. We may sometimes despair of the possibility of a hospitable planet. And it may be too late. But even if it is, and we are in inevitable decline toward a scarcely habitable earth, there is time and space for hospitality when it can be made, and for the happiness and satisfaction of its structures of living. If the sad scenarios of the semi-desert and decimated population of a planet whose energy is forever damaged are fulfilled, then, too, hospitality with what is left will be our only hope of remaining human and loving in contrast to the solution of total regimentation for the control of scarce resources which is sketched by the "Terran" ambassador in Le Guin's *The Dispossessed.* Yet the doom is not inevitable, and there are indeed signs of a change in hearts and hands. Though it is not thought of in terms of hospitality, new ways of thinking about and structuring organization, for instance, show a new respect for that fluidity of roles, for that redefinition of ownership and that willingness to share both information and decision making that hospitality implies.

The thinking behind this has been at first fairly pragmatic in terms of the fact that people who are treated as responsible contributors work better, and that the pooling of insights and experience leads to the development of better ways to do things. But more recently the beneficial way such things work in practice has been connected to the changed cosmology that bears with it the possibility of liberating us from the mental and spiritual prison of a mechanistic, dualistic universe into one that expresses itself as a dance of dynamic interdependence at the micro and the macro level, and in which the very boundaries between spiritual and material melt, allowing the emergence of new forms of living.

This has happened because people concerned with human organizational structures have begun to apply to them the insights of physicists who, in this century, have revolutionized our perception of reality. What began as an esoteric conversation between scientists spilled over some decades ago when scientists who were also philosophers, such as Fritjof Capra, perceived a whole new way of thinking about human as well as sub-atomic organization. Capra's books, *The Tao of Physics* and *The Turning Point,* and other books in the same vein gave currency (and comprehensibility) to scientific observations with mind-blowing implications. Later, what came to be known as "chaos theory" persuaded organizational experts to recognize that order is not something that has to be imposed by the Divine Surrogates (with constant observations, recordings, bribes and sanctions to keep it under control) but rather something that needs to be released and discovered throughout the organism, as it is in nature.

The insights of modern science and the new cosmology to which it gives birth have been mentioned earlier in the book. There are finally two concepts drawn from modern physics that help to illuminate the idea that hospitality is more than a generous impulse that can help to mitigate the inevitable brutality of "normal" social organization.

One is Prigogine's phrase, "dissipative structures." "Dissipation" is about loss, it is a process by which energy gradually lessens and disappears, but Prigogine showed that this dissipative action actually has to do with the creation of new structures. Rather than spelling the inevitable end of a system it allows the system to let go of what is no longer needed and recreate itself in a way that fits its environment better. That sounds like an encouraging thought for human structures at the end of the twentieth century. There is no inevitable entropy—the machine running down—but rather an organism with an inherent ability to take on new forms without losing its identity. However, in the case of the human communal organism this can only happen through human choices, and hospitality is such a choice.

Hospitality means letting go of total control of the environment. Rather than guarding our spaces from the foes—the terrifying neediness of more than half the world, the possibility of the imposed necessity of a radically changed lifestyle such as Le Guin evokes fictionally—we recognize that the higher we build our barriers the less the life-quality we can conserve. Entropy overtakes the carefully preserved structures, but hospitality—to new ideas, new ways of relating, governing, educating, farming, traveling—can renew the spaces, bringing in a sense of hope, comradeship, meaning. It does not destroy what has been precious but calls us to experience our inheritance in new ways, interpreted through the vision of hospitality.

Lewis Thomas, the biologist, once observed that when he heard people laughing in an experimental laboratory, saying, "that's preposterous," it meant that shortly something really worthwhile would be emerging. That extraordinary shift of consciousness that suddenly makes "normal" reality look quite different is a kind of liberation from the expected that feels *funny*. Nobody, in the controlled and defended structures of the Divine Surrogates, laughs very much, except perhaps for the sycophantic giggle of the survivors when a non-conformist has been expelled.

The other concept that helps us to understand how hospitality can work in theory and practice is that of the aptly named "strange attractor." It is something that we can't perceive unless we let go the conviction that everything important that appears is in a straight line of cause and effect and that everything around or beyond that is irrelevant and needs to be discounted, even if it may be beautiful or beneficial or dangerous. Since what is not linear can't be predicted or controlled, it has been disregarded by science and therefore by people trying to create human systems on what they thought of as scientific principles. So art and grief and the pattern of clouds and the laughter of children and tornadoes and dreams and riots were left out of the calculations, though in practice they could and did drastically disturb the results.

Chaos theory has changed all that, and computers have allowed us to "map" the shape of phenomena that we had assumed to be so arbitrary that no "meaning" could be found in them. Scientists have been able to track the evolution of a "chaotic" system with computers, in what is called "phase space" that allows the observer to see a system's movement in many dimensions, a moment in the system's state being encoded as a point of light on the screen. A computer can do this so fast that something that could never have been observed by "ordinary" vision becomes visible. The "chaotic" state of a system that has moved away from equilibrium is tracked, and at first it seems as unpredictable as we would expect—it dashes about all over the place, never twice in the same place. But after a while a pattern begins to emerge, because these crazy gyrations are always within a boundary. Gradually, marvelous forms are created on the screen—a butterfly shape, or a strange three-winged bird-like form. Chaos, thus observed, is orderly yet unpredictable, and its endless iterations create magical images that can come to symbolize the possibility of experiencing reality in entirely new ways—yet in ways that were going on, were basic to the nature of reality, long before computers were invented to allow people to perceive them or even before there were people to do the perceiving. Gaia, the earth, solid and shapely, was born of Chaos—endless, unorganized possibility—and all else was born from the womb of Gaia. She represents those strange unimposed boundaries of chaos, giving meaning and beauty.

Hospitality is what chaos physics calls a "strange attractor." It provides the mysterious boundaries within which the systems of healthy human and earthly interaction can follow their unpredictable yet orderly dance. Hospitality of its nature is not controllable, yet it is not disorderly. It evades the equilibrium of an idealized continuity that is actually decay, it is inherently surprising because once thresholds are no longer impermeable anyone or anything can come in, yet the coming in is part of the pattern; it is not an invasion but a new figure in the dance. As it is repeated and repeated the pattern becomes clearer, and the symbolic shape it describes becomes more easily recognizable as expressing an awesome and joyful reality, a reference point for choices, an image of the immanent and yet transcendent divinity.

A strange attractor is the result and symbol of open systems, unpredictable yet orderly, constantly changing yet with a pattern of meaning. The computer-generated pattern is a visual image of that openness, which yet has its own boundaries, boundaries not imposed but created by its own nature.

What can this mean for us in terms of transformation of our lives, the spaces of our living?

It seems possible that the practice (principle? experience? criterion? law?) of hospitality, and its marvelous symbol, the strange attractor, are for us a myth structure than we can use. The very word *hospitality* immediately conjures up stories—stories of Olympian beings entertained by poor peasantry, of Abraham in the desert, of the widow of Sarephtha, of Scrooge's change of heart; there are innumerable stories from folk tales and from real life of the poor sharing their homes and goods, or of homes opened to fleeing slaves or other refugees from oppression. There are also the stories that warn about the abuse of the tradition of hospitality, like the witch who invites Hansel and Gretel into her cottage with offers of sugarplums, of Snow White's stepmother playing on her curiosity and compassion to get into her house and kill her, or stories (all too observable in real life) of the wealthy using a false hospitality to impress or persuade. The myth of hospitality is universal, and powerful. It is inherent also in religious reflection, even in the Christian doctrine of incarnation whereby God enters the human habitation and shares the human home, and is welcomed by some and rejected by others. It is present in the image of Jesus who talks about his "Father's house" where there is room for all, yet some exclude themselves by their own choice. The myth is present in the Jewish ritual of Passover, at which the hope of the coming of the Messiah is traditionally symbolized by setting a place at the table for Elijah, the wandering prophet who will return to precede the Messiah.

A myth takes form in such stories because it is a guiding principle, one that is even felt to be a determining criterion of human value. To practice hospitality is to be "righteous," to refuse hospitality or to abuse it is to become, in some sense, incapable of human community, outcast and alien.

If hospitality is the myth that guides and judges, then we need to look at all ours structures in relation to that. We need to look at our most literal structures, our buildings, and see if they are "permeable" in the sense of facilitating hospitality. Do our banks look as if *anyone* were welcome to get help and advice about the use of their earnings? Are our schools and universities built (literally and metaphorically) to encourage the sharing of knowledge rather than the channeling of information?

What does a hospitable household consist of ? Hospitality requires flexibility of roles, adaptability of spaces, a letting go of anxiety about possession. Mothers, fathers, siblings, friends, exchange functions and roles as new challenges appear on the threshold.

Hospitality changes town planning, urging values of neighborhood, creating common spaces and shared facilities and services. It turns churches into beautiful multi-purpose spaces and touches every structure with sacredness because the guest is always sacred and we are all guests.

Hospitality involves risk but it also creates meaning. The hospitable community has a focus beyond itself; it perceives the divine guest in every human, every animal, every bird and fish and insect, plant and pond and tree and cloud. "Earthed" by the images of hospitality in use in actual structures—houses and schools and offices and gardens and farms and wilderness areas and shores and political boundaries—we are able to deal more realistically and practically with the notions of hospitality operating in structures that are not material in that obvious sense yet closely connected to it: political and economic structures, philosophical and linguistic structures, and the structures that, in practice, control minds such as historical and scientific ones and usually religious and artistic ones.

As this book demonstrates, an unease that leads to questioning of the meaning of any of these—including the actual spaces of daily living whose forms are in turn dictated by these other structures—has arisen, and philosophers, linguists, economists, historians, scientists, artists and even politicians and business people have opened magic casements and leaned out, have breathed in a different air, have felt the spray of other seas and looked on previously unimagined landscapes. Not many of them have expressed in terms of hospitality what they saw in contrast to what they were supposed to see, but the critiques they have developed, the (occasionally wild) experiments they have conducted, and the visions they have proposed can be perceived to relate to hospitality as the moral criterion for structural choices. These choices are spiritual choices, and in a sense all choices are spiritual, since they express a person's or a community's basic convictions. Hospitality as a criterion can only work if it is based on spiritual conviction that must, at this time, run counter to the prevailing ideology, as the convictions of the Chambonnais ran counter to the demands of the occupying forces as well as the moral inertia of many fellow citizens.

The spiritual nature of hospitality is inherent. In a hospitable system we cannot regard spirituality as a kind of icing on the cake of whatever economic and social systems are current, to sweeten and soften them, or as an escape from the harshness of reality. This is so because it is impossible, in practice, to create hospitable systems without the double vision that perceives old and new, myths and material reality, at one time. It is impossible without the anachronism that breaks out in the thresholds of changed spaces because hospitality is in practice too risky unless the conviction of the existence and overriding importance of that moral imperative drives the choices that we make. Hospitality is impossible without that sense of permeability that transforms perception of possibility.

In Chapter 4 I looked at the significance of the regions under the floor of conscious daily life in terms of baptism, and suggested that redesigned structures need to allow for periodic return to those places of beginning, the womb from which consciousness emerges. Hospitality has to be founded in that sense of origins, making choices and decisions on the basis of an awareness of the ambiguity and danger of the depths in each person and in the community. The fear of the depths is a proper fear, a challenge to accept the "lower" in ourselves as integral, and powerful and, as the symbols of baptism imply, potentially sacred. But if we refuse this baptism, the fear of the unknown depths is transferred to people who are "different," who carry the threat of an "otherness" we can't control. We dare not be hospitable to them; our structures must limit hospitality to those who are "like us," and that category shrinks and shrinks. Baptism in the sense explored in that chapter, therefore, is a pre-condition of a vision of earthly life that makes it possible to break down barriers.

As we saw, however, the breaking of barriers is not enough. Hospitality modifies the use and design of spaces but it cannot exist without them. The exits and entrances are real, even though they may change their significance in revolutionary ways. This need for boundaries, even though changed ones, is the biggest practical and spiritual problem for the use of hospitality as a moral criterion, in a way that is very familiar in political issues concerning refugees and immigration at national levels, and at local levels of attitudes to "incomers." It is familiar, too, in the need for "security" systems and the fear of strangers. *Hospitality* in the sense developed here, therefore, depends on the awareness that there are other "stages," that the exits from our particular "stage" may be not backstage but onto another stage, another culture, and that the hospitable choice may have to do less with inviting the audience to share the show or inviting the stagehands to take a bow and more with being aware of and respectful and even financially supportive of audience and back stage technicians and scene shifters who may be the significant actors on that other stage that is not seen. This is a shift in moral perception both of ourselves and "other" kinds of people that is difficult and not popular with governments (national or local), because these depend on persuading the electorate that the only criterion for voting for one party or another is the degree of personal material advantage each can provide or pretend to provide for the voter.

Connected to this, the perceived value to the community of a particular group of people—women, for instance, and categories of occupation such as farmers or soldiers—is changed, "upward" and "downward." The spaces they occupy, in buildings or in the economy or in public awareness, are changed, and this is very threatening when it means, as it does, that others are displaced. Rethinking these group valuations in terms of hospitality rather than competition means that kind of awareness of the sacred significance of thresholds and the power that is in them. An exit, at first sight a "downgrading," can be an entrance somewhere else.

However if some painful, problematic and openly heretical (in terms of the dominant orthodoxy) choices are to be made, the element of revolution must not be pursued at the expense of the equally important criterion of continuity, which easily happens because continuity is less controversial, or appears to be. The purpose of hospitality as a criterion is, in a sense, to ensure continuity, even across thresholds, for without it the people lose identity and, with it, the strength and self-respect that make possible the adaptability to change. Tradition is what supports immigrants in a new land; tradition is in the education of the artist whose trained eye and sensitized perception give confidence to move to radical images and techniques. Tradition that bears centuries of experience of religious symbols is what makes possible the rediscovery of the meaning of the sacred in daily life. Hospitality as a concept draws its power and realism for a tradition as old as human records and no doubt older.

The houses of our lives have been built and knocked down and built again on top of the old or elsewhere, or redesigned in ways that at first sight deny continuity, yet the simplest history of architecture—or philosophy or education or social structures—shows how, taking a long view, changes have grown out of what was there before, if only in reaction. Also, over and over again, styles have changed by reviving old ones—but always with significant differences. Hospitality cannot be exercised as if we were desert nomads or medieval monks, but the tradition draws on those memories. As a moral criterion for the world now, it requires both a sense of that long history and also new kinds of awareness, new kinds of knowledge and new skills that are only available at this point in history.

At the risk of repeating myself it needs to be said that hospitality is a criterion for moral choices which can only be made out of a profound and sensitive spiritual awareness that draws on ancient myths and symbols but knows how to risk new languages of structure to embody them. It requires a strong and clear sense of spiritual reality to apply such a moral criterion, and it also requires freedom of imagination and freedom of what can only be called *translation* of inherited symbols, a translation that can recognize the power of the tradition at work in decisions that make use of new insight.

It is not the main purpose of this book to propose practical applications of the concept of hospitality as a moral criterion, although examples and stories have been used to pin down the theory in terms of imaginable reality. The image of a house in dire need of repair, of adaptation and changes of spatial relationships, has been used to keep that focus on the coincidence of the spiritual and the practical, and the practical as spiritual. All the examples (magic casements, stage exits and entrances, the concept of permeability and more) have been used in the hope of evoking a sense of possibility, in which tradition and change are functionally interrelated and choices can be made at micro and macro levels that are both visionary and realistic. Whether we are talking about the choices of individual lifestyle, of household roles and structures, of the design of homes and churches and schools and clinics and farms, of villages and towns, of educational structures and priorities, of neighborhood organizations or agricultural and land-policy, of immigration and overseas aid policies, of penal systems, of health care (national and—desirably—local), we are talking about interrelated structural choices in which hospitality as a criterion not only can but must, if humans are to survive on earth, govern our choices.

Life—human life and all earthly life—needs continuity and stability, and also needs vision and adaptability. The structures must change and adapt, but this must not be a panic adaptation or an enforced change, and if we use hospitality as our image it will be something that happens because the deepest nature of creatures requires it. Responding to that requirement gives meaning and purpose; there is room for courage but also for quiet contentment, for high achievement but also for satisfaction in the everyday, for rhythm and succession and the cycles of seasons and lives. And, finally, language itself, freed from the need to be either totally and blindly identified with one culture (like the people who tried to build the tower of Babel) or completely fluid and without developed word-thing relationships, can be hospitable to meanings learned from other cultures, able to welcome newcomers without being dominated by "newspeak." It can have the humility that knows the constantly changing nature of the language and yet rejoices in the continuities that link us to former generations and the richness of past associations. And—strangest of all, perhaps—the very attempt to treat language with respect and humility, as neither master nor slave but as both tool and teacher, soon begins to change the shapes of other structures, making them also more hospitable.

All this can sound romantic and far from practical decision making, but, as this book has suggested, the tide of new—and very old—imagination is already flowing and new ways are being used successfully, new structures built, new spaces created, that are hospitable, and therefore full of meaning and the energy that happens when meaning is perceived.

The entropy of our civilization—far advanced as it appears—can be reversed. Much has been lost and undoubtedly much more will be lost, and perhaps this earth will never again be the beautiful, fertile place that once it was. But life will go on, and whatever of creativity and fertility can be salvaged will depend on the survival, also, of a spirit of hospitality. If our earth survives as a place for human life to flourish, even in a diminished world, it will be because, however reluctantly, the structures of greed and dominance have been forced to acknowledge the necessity of the principle of hospitality, though they are unlikely to name it in that way. Models are needed and are emerging that, like Le Chambon, say that it can be done. Reclaiming the spaces of living as places of hospitality for all things living is not an ideal, it is the basic condition of survival. And it is not something that will happen because governments become more enlightened, or businesses engage in corporate reorganizing in order to become more efficient. On the contrary, the structures of government and business and education and religion will only change if they are peopled by those who share the vision of hospitality. It must begin in the wonder and sacredness of ordinary people, the people who have learned to imagine and gone on to take energetic steps to make a home.

Keatz- 54

Kruee - 103
   127
   128 (permeable5)

141-
Burnett - 151
D. Cornes - 158
    160
Percy - 163
LeGuin - 163
Day - 170

Cortos b Reffuse -
Nuw/reut

"dissapalive structures" (Prigscine)